AF605855

CLASSICS IN CALIFORNIA ANTHROPOLOGY

CARVING TRADITIONS OF NORTHWEST CALIFORNIA

Carving Traditions of Northwest California

Ira Jacknis

With a Reprint of

THE CARVER'S ART
OF THE INDIANS OF
NORTHWESTERN CALIFORNIA

by Isabel T. Kelly

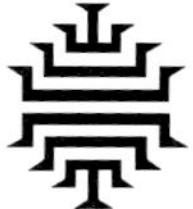

PHOEBE HEARST MUSEUM OF ANTHROPOLOGY
UNIVERSITY OF CALIFORNIA, BERKELEY

Editor: Ira Jacknis
Project Manager: Barbara Takiguchi
Designer: Sarah Levin
Printer: Publishers Press, United States of America
10 9 8 7 6 5 4 3 2 1

This publication was made possible with the generous support of the California Council for the Humanities, the Fleishhacker Foundation, and the LEF Foundation.

The paper used in this publication meets the minimum requirements of American National Standard for Information Sciences—Permanence of Paper for Printed Materials, ANSI Z39.48–1984.

Unless otherwise noted, all photographs are of Hearst Museum objects (identified by "1–catalogue number") and were taken by Eugene Prince, Hearst Museum photographer.

Cover photo: Dugout canoe moored to the shore of the Trinity River at Hostler Ranch, Hoopa Valley, California. Photograph by Pliny E. Goddard, 1902 (neg. no. 15–3342).

Portions of *Carving Traditions of Northwest California* by Ira Jacknis appeared in *American Indian Art Magazine*, volume 20, number 4 (1995).

LIBRARY OF CONGRESS CATALOGING-IN-PUBLICATION DATA:
Jacknis, Ira.
Carving traditions of northwest California / Ira Jacknis.
With a reprint of The carver's art of the Indians of northwestern California / by Isabel T. Kelly.
p. cm. — (Classics in California anthropology)
Second work originally published: Berkeley : University of California Press, 1930, in series: University of California publications in American archaeology and ethnology ; v. 24, no. 7.
Includes bibliographical references.
ISBN 0-936127-05-8 (alk. paper)
1. Indian wood-carving—California. 2. Indian wood-carving—Klamath River Valley (Or. and Calif.) 3. Indian art—Klamath River Valley (Or. and Calif.) 4. Indians of North America—Klamath River Valley (Or. and Calif.) 5.Wood-carving—Klamath River Valley (Or. and Calif.)—Patterns. 6. Klamath River Valley (Or. and Calif.)—Antiquities. I. Kelly, Isabel Truesdell, 1906-Carver's art of the Indians of northwestern California. II. Title. III. Title: Carver's art of the Indians of northwestern California. IV. Series.
E78.C15J315 1995
730'.089'9707941—dc 95-24814
CIP

Copyright © 1995 by The Regents of the University of California. All rights reserved. Reproduction or use, without written permission, of editorial or pictorial content in any manner is prohibited.

PHOEBE APPERSON HEARST MUSEUM OF ANTHROPOLOGY
103 Kroeber Hall
University of California
Berkeley, California 94720

CONTENTS

ACKNOWLEDGMENTS

First, I want to thank my two co-curators, George Blake and Frank Gist. Curatorial consultation was facilitated by a grant from the California Humanities Council. Next, I would like to thank my research assistant, Robin DeLugan, graduate student in anthropology at UC Berkeley. For helpful conversations and comments, I thank Allan Bramlette, Victor Golla, David Hostler, Rosemary Joyce, Malcolm Margolin, Margaret Mathewson, Martha Muhs, Steven Shackley, and Barbara Takiguchi. I am especially grateful to Thomas Buckley, Coleen Kelley Marks, and Beverly R. Ortiz for their careful reading of the manuscript. Ruth Flaxman was the copyeditor. I, of course, remain responsible for all errors and misinterpretations. I first had the opportunity to interview George Blake in 1990, while working at The Brooklyn Museum, New York, in a project supported by the National Endowment for the Humanities.

Ira Jacknis

CLASSICS IN CALIFORNIA ANTHROPOLOGY:

Introduction to the Hearst Museum Reprint Series

The Phoebe Apperson Hearst Museum of Anthropology seeks to preserve its collections and improve their documentation and accessibility, sponsors research on its collections, and presents research relevant to its collections and mission in the form of publications, programs, and exhibitions. The museum recognizes a special responsibility as a repository of perhaps the largest collection in North America of the material culture produced by the Indians of California. With the inauguration of a series of reprints on Native California, the museum seeks to fulfill its commitment to making knowledge about Native California more widely accessible.

The series initiates a new chapter in the long and distinguished history of publications of anthropological research from Berkeley. Prominent among these are the studies produced by researchers from the Anthropology Department and Museum of Anthropology, published in the series University of California Publications in American Archaeology and Ethnology (UCPAAE). Volume one, number one of the UCPAAE, *Life and Culture of the Hupa* by Pliny Goddard, marked the strong focus on California that would characterize the entire series.

The UCPAAE was initiated in 1903 with the financial support of Phoebe Apperson Hearst, and was modeled on the annual reports and bulletins of the Smithsonian Institution's Bureau of American Ethnology. Like BAE publications, the UCPAAE volumes were not for sale to the general public but were exchanged with libraries and scholars. Studies varied in length from long articles to monographs of several hundred pages. In 1937, a second series was added, called Anthropological Records. According to a publisher's note, the UCPAAE was "restricted to papers in which the interpretative element outweighs the factual or which otherwise are of general interest." The new series was "issued in photolithography in a larger size. It consists of monographs which are documentary, of record nature, or devoted to the presentation primarily of new data." In 1964, the series Publications in Anthropology superseded the UCPAAE. By then, fifty volumes subdivided into 237 separate numbers had been published in the UCPAAE. The vast majority of original research from Berkeley about California Indians was published in the three series. Today, almost all of these important works are out of print.

Classics in California Anthropology will present selected volumes from these series and other older sources, enhanced with new introductions by contemporary scholars and, when appropriate, additional illustrations. We intend that Classics in California Anthropology will make available to new audiences landmark works created by a pioneering generation of anthropologists.

Rosemary A. Joyce, Director
May 1995

PREFACE

This photographic reprinting of Isabel Kelly's classic 1930 study of the carving traditions of the Klamath River Indians from Northwest California is occasioned by a comprehensive exhibition (August 23, 1995–February 4, 1996) of this material at the Phoebe Hearst Museum of Anthropology (formerly the Lowie Museum) at the University of California, Berkeley. This supplemental introduction covers objects she omitted (such as pipes and canoes), issues she did not cover (such as construction techniques and uses), and an update reviewing the contemporary situation.

Alfred Kroeber, the original collector and student of so many of these objects, perceived Klamath River cultures as vanishing, and these peoples did suffer greatly from genocide, disease, and forced acculturation. In recent years, however, there has been a significant revival of traditional Klamath River culture, including various forms of carving. The exhibition includes the objects and expertise of two of the region's most noted contemporary carvers—George Blake (Hupa/Yurok) and Frank Gist (Yurok). In addition to working in a range of traditional forms, Blake and Gist have extended the tradition. Both have adapted traditional materials like elk antler and traditional shapes like the spoon in a variety of carved jewelry, and over the last decade, George Blake has produced innovative, nonfunctional forms which are intended as sculpture. Between October 1994 and April 1995, both carvers commented on the construction, form, and uses of the carvings in the Hearst Museum collections. They have also suggested the appropriate exhibition themes, helped select the objects, and offered commentary on the pieces.[1]

The exhibition, along with this introduction, addresses issues of aesthetic anthropology. Taking our cue from Kelly's original title, its focus is on the carver's art: what carving was in the Klamath River area of Northwestern California at the turn of the century, and how, why, and for whom it was created. Weaving together diverse sources from the published literature, archival fieldnotes, museum collections, and my contemporary interviews and observations, I have attempted to sketch out a basic art history for Klamath River carving, a task that is long overdue. Although much new information is presented, more research can and should be done. This essay represents a beginning.

Ira Jacknis
Associate Research Anthropologist

CARVING TRADITIONS OF NORTHWEST CALIFORNIA

by Ira Jacknis

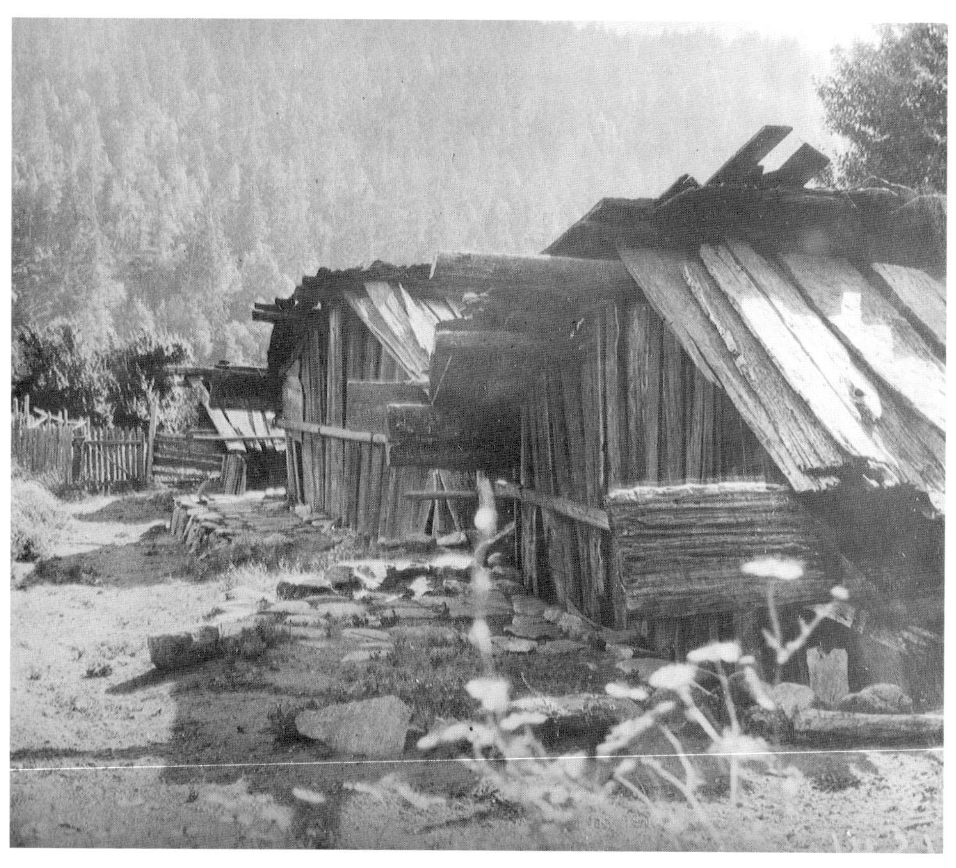

Wahsekw, a Yurok village.
Photograph by Alfred Kroeber, 1907 (neg. no. 15–1421).

THE CULTURAL CONTEXT

The peoples of the Klamath River region—the Yurok, Hupa, Karuk, Tolowa, and other groups—possessed the most elaborate carving tradition of Native California. Carved objects of wood, elk antler, and stone played an important role in much of their culture. The southernmost extension of the status- and wealth-conscious cultures of the Northwest Coast region (British Columbia and Alaska), these societies were distinguished by rank and wealth and inherited privilege, similar to European aristocracies (Pilling 1978:141, 1989). As on the Northwest Coast, they derived much of their subsistence from fishing, supplementing the more central Californian nutritional base of acorns and other plant foods. Like the more northerly region, too, their carving was highly developed, both in quantity and in complexity. Both regions erected large plank houses, which formed the foundation for woodworking skills. Klamath River groups preserved valued dance regalia in redwood chests and dentalium shell money in similarly shaped elk antler purses. While other Native Californians also used wooden paddles to cook acorn mush, only the Klamath River groups carved the handles in intricate patterns, and they were the only Californian peoples to have household furniture such as wooden pillows and stools (Kroeber 1925:92).

The relations among the Klamath River groups are complex. Although speaking languages of three distinct families, these cultures carried on extensive intertribal communication and trade. There are some important differences between these cultures—important especially to the people themselves—but they tended to be quite similar in their material aspects. As one anthropologist put it: "The cultural homogeneity of this region was perhaps most pronounced in the realm of material culture,...and the wide array of tools used for hunting, fishing, woodworking, and other crafts was virtually identical among these groups" (Gould 1978:130, see also Elsasser 1978:161). One of the biggest differences is that canoes were made only by the coastal Tolowa, Yurok, and Wiyot, where the redwood grew, and traded to the upriver Hupa and Karuk. The southern Athapaskan groups (Mattole, Nongatl, Sinkyone, Lassik, Wailaki) shared some traits with lower Klamath River peoples, but in other ways they were quite distinct. For instance, except for the Mattole, their houses were generally round. To date, no clear tribal style has been determined for carved objects such as spoons, mush paddles, or purses.

Our knowledge of these groups is uneven. Most of our written sources concern the Yurok, largely because of Alfred Kroeber's six decades of research devoted to them. Also because of Kroeber, the Hearst Museum collections from the region are also predominantly Yurok. Another factor for this ethnographic representation may have been their greater numbers. Although we have no accurate counts, population estimates for 1848 place the Yurok at about 3000, with the Karuk and the Hupa around 2700 and 1000, respectively.

Our temporal sources are also limited, as there has been very little archaeological investigation of this region (Frederickson 1984). Most Klamath River groups traditionally trace their origin and historical development within their current homelands. Archaeologists and linguists have hypothesized successive migrations. They believe that ancestors of the Karuk (Hokan-speakers) may have been the earliest of present-day peoples to settle in the area. According to this view, around A.D. 900, ancestral Wiyots (Algonquian-speakers) first brought to the Klamath River region the characteristic cultural complex from the north—an elaborate technology based on riverine fishing and woodworking, and a wealth-consciousness as expressed in large obsidian blades and dentalium shell beads. The related Yurok groups, also from the north, arrived about 1100, with the Hupa and other Athapaskan groups coming about 1300. Soil types and climatic conditions are not very suitable for the preservation of organic materials, but some carved objects of bone (netting needles, awls, harpoon heads) and stone (net sinkers, projectile points, pipes, bowls) have survived from the so-called Gunther Pattern. Although there is little or no surviving wood, the characteristic set of woodworking tools (antler wedges, stone mauls and adzes) is present. One of the earliest elk antler spoons recovered dates back to the period 1620–1775 (Elsasser and Heizer 1966:95, pl. 24e).

The peoples of this region had relatively little interaction with Europeans for many years after initial contact. The Spanish may have visited the Yurok as early as 1565, but there was no documented contact until 1775. For most of these groups, especially those inland from the coast, the period for which we have the most detailed information, the so-called "ethnographic present," begins about 1850, when gold was discovered in the Trinity Mountains area. Because so many of the sources anthropologists have created and used apply to the period between about 1850 and 1920, this time has, unfortunately, been reified as the "traditional period," as if Klamath River people had always lived this way. Everything that we know suggests that the Yurok, Hupa, Karuk, and their neighbors have always adapted to the world as they found it. The present study attempts to place their carving into evolving traditions instead of fixing them in a lost "golden age" (for an African case, see Steiner 1994:100–29).

THE HISTORY OF COLLECTION AND STUDY

The carving of the Klamath River Indians was mentioned in passing by early travelers between 1775 and the 1850s (see Heizer and Mills 1952), but it was not described in any depth until the surveys of journalist Stephen Powers. In 1877 Powers published *Tribes of California,* incorporating reports of his 1871–72 visit and his 1875–76 return on a commission to make a modest collection and report for the Centennial Exposition. This collection, subsequently accessioned by the Smithsonian's National Museum, was supplemented by a Hupa collection gathered by Army Lieutenant P. Henry Ray. The 1889 essay on the Ray collection by curator Otis Mason was the first scholarly analysis of Klamath River material culture. Following this, however, there was no systematic anthropological study until the end of the century.

In the summer of 1900, Alfred L. Kroeber (1876–1960) first visited Northwest California, a region that would remain the focus of his scholarly life until his death. After less than a year as a curator for San Francisco's California Academy of Sciences, he resigned due to their lack of support for research. In September of the following year,

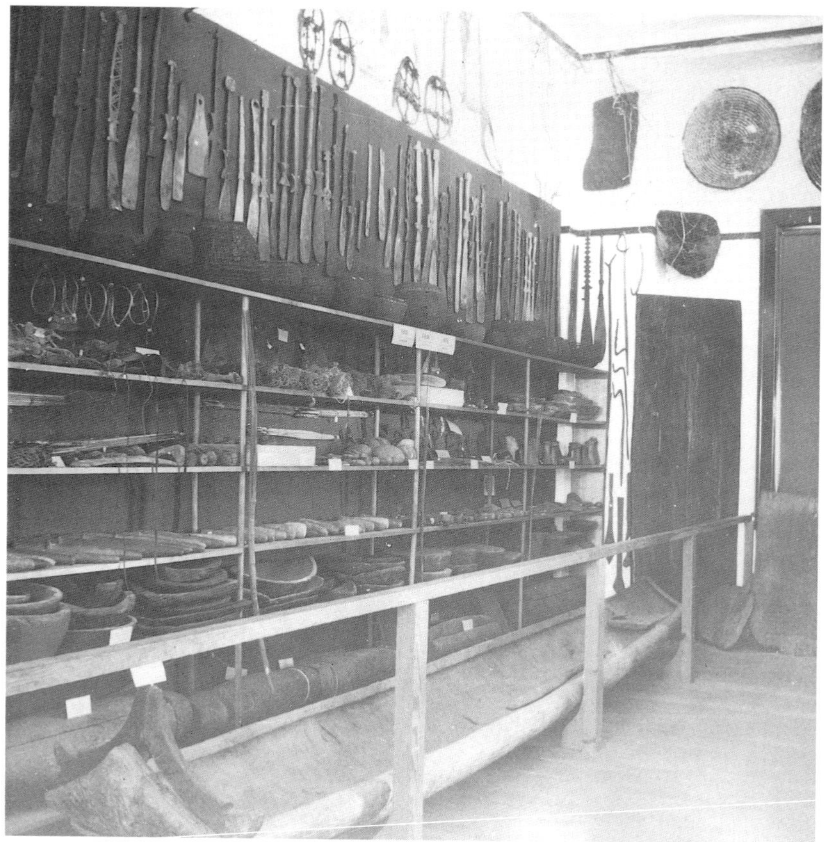

Klamath River carvings in the Museum of Anthropology,
University of California, San Francisco.
Photograph by Alfred Kroeber, 1907 (neg. no. 15–4205).

Kroeber returned as the first curator of the new anthropology museum at the University of California. Along with his colleagues and students, he tirelessly gathered artifacts and documented the Native cultures of California. During this first decade, Kroeber spent much of his time in the field, collecting for the University museum (Thoresen 1976, Jacknis 1993). He was so industrious in his attempt to make a "complete" tribal collection that he nearly succeeded in collecting at least one example of every item of "traditional" manufacture for the Yurok. Although he was in a position to see many of these objects in use, Kroeber seems to have recorded no eyewitness accounts of artifact construction. His information was probably based on Native memories of practices during the early contact period, c. 1850. Consequently, there is much we do not know about these objects. Alfred Kroeber summarized these years of collaborative research in his comprehensive *Handbook of the Indians of California* (1925). Its chapter on Yurok material culture remains the best introduction to Klamath River carving (1925:76–97).

Even before Kroeber's arrival, however, the University museum had been collecting in this region. The Museum's founder, Phoebe Hearst, had personally employed Dr. Philip Mills Jones, a physician by training, to gather archaeological and ethnographic material from California and adjacent states. During two weeks in the summer of 1901, Jones managed to secure a relatively large and comprehensive Klamath River collection, focusing on the Hupa.

In addition to acquisitions directly from Native peoples, Jones and Kroeber made indirect purchases from a thriving secondary market in the area. The focus of this trade was the merchant Alexander Brizard, who operated with his family a series of general stores in Arcata, Hoopa, Weitchpec, Somes Bar, and Orleans (Jacknis 1991:163). Around 1900 Brizard began to make a reputation as a dealer in Indian artifacts and a supplier to private and institutional collectors. While he concentrated on baskets, Brizard included carvings and regalia among his wares. One of the suppliers to the Museum was Frank Gist, an ancestor of the contemporary carver of the same name, who was also a purchasing agent for Brizard (Jacknis 1991:181–82).

In his study of Klamath River peoples, Kroeber was assisted by numerous students and colleagues,[2] but the one most relevant to our story here was Isabel Kelly (1906–82). A native of Santa Cruz, California, Isabel Truesdell Kelly was influenced by her aunt, who often traveled abroad with her nieces; at the age of nineteen, she visited Bolivia on one of these trips. Upon entering the University of California at Berkeley as a physical education major, Kelly enrolled in an anthropology course due to an entanglement of academic bureaucracy. She liked the course so much that she decided to become an anthropologist, earning her bachelor's degree in 1926 and her master's the following year.

It was Kroeber who assigned Kelly the topic of her master's paper—the carving of the Klamath River Indians (Buzaljko 1993:43). He had been thinking about the Museum's collection of spoons and mush paddles and was looking for someone to study them. Kelly's formal analysis was based strictly on the Museum's collection. In the absence of personal contact with Native people, she cited Kroeber's Yurok informant Robert Johnson.[3] Despite its limitations, Kelly's work remains the only extended analysis of Klamath River carving beyond Kroeber's summary in the *Handbook*. The carving essay was one of three museum projects that Kelly worked on in her graduate years. The others were on Peruvian pottery and Yuki basketry, all three published in the University's anthropological series (Kelly 1930a, b, c). Before leaving Berkeley, Kelly spent six months in late 1931 and early 1932 investigating the Coast Miwok, in nearby Marin County, supplying us with much of the basic ethnography of these people (Collier and Thalman 1991). Because Kroeber discouraged his graduate students from working in archaeology, her true passion, Kelly earned her doctorate in 1932 with a dissertation on Great Basin ethnography. She went on to a distinguished career as an archaeologist of Western Mexico, in addition to important work in Southwestern archaeology, Plains Indian ethnography, international public health, and Mexican social anthropology (Knobloch 1988).

In subsequent years, the Museum made very few accessions of Klamath River carving, similar to the pattern for the regalia but different from the acquisitions of baskets, which continued to come in over the decades through the gifts of private collectors (Jacknis 1994:3). The principal exception to this trend was the small, but important, field research, collecting, and filming by Samuel A. Barrett in 1960. The first to earn a doctorate in anthropology from the University of California, in 1908, Barrett returned to his alma mater in 1953 after a long career at the Milwaukee Public Museum. Among his many projects, Barrett set out to work with his mentor on the preparation of comprehensive summaries of Northwestern California material culture. While the volume on fishing was published (Kroeber and Barrett 1960), unfortunately the one on woodcarving (Barrett, et al. ms.) was left incomplete with the deaths of Kroeber in 1960 and

Barrett in 1965. Klamath River carving was included in Barrett's other major retirement project—the American Indian Film Project (1961a). In an attempt to record as much as he could of what he perceived to be "vanishing cultures," Barrett produced a series of fifteen films between 1961 and 1965. In addition to one on Tolowa arrowpoint-making was a record of the construction of a Yurok sinew-backed bow and arrow set (1961b) and unreleased footage of canoe and elk antler spoon carving. Along with the photography, Barrett made modest collections, offering us a valuable record of carving at this time.

The Phoebe Hearst Museum has perhaps the world's largest and most comprehensive collection of carvings from this region.[4] Like the Museum's collection of dance regalia from the Klamath River, almost all the carving from this region arrived in the Museum's first decade (especially in the years 1901–02 and 1906–07), and, again, the two principal collectors were Kroeber and Jones. As indicated, it is richest in both variety and numbers of items for the Yurok. For instance, there are eighty-one Yurok elk antler spoons compared to twenty-four from the Hupa and none from the Karuk. Similarly, for purses, the proportions are thirty-eight Yurok, seven Hupa, one Tolowa, and no Karuk. Kroeber collected all the fifty-eight Yurok mush paddles; P. M. Jones acquired most of the ten Hupa examples. One of the larger categories is pipes; here there are more Hupa pieces, twenty-three, than Yurok, fifteen. Together, spoons, paddles, purses, and pipes are the largest categories of carved objects from the region in the Hearst collections. There are smaller numbers of the storage boxes, canoes, paddles, house parts, ladders, stools, pillows, dishes, tools, and other miscellaneous items.

Many factors, as yet unstudied, might explain the presence of so many of these objects in museum collections. Like the Pomo, for example (Smith-Ferri 1993), the Yurok and their neighbors took an active role in yielding up their crafts to white collectors. As P. M. Jones noted "These Indians are getting very commercial and in many cases ask the full value and more, for some things" (1901). Another possible explanation may have been the decline in Native populations. For example, although precise numbers are lacking, according to estimates the Hupa population declined from a high of 1000 individuals in 1851 to 420 in 1906, when anthropologists and others were actively collecting their objects (Wallace 1978:176). As in the case of Northwest Coast carving, the depopulation of the late nineteenth century meant that there were fewer Native people who needed these objects, and, with culture change and a shift to Euroamerican material culture, less need for these kinds of items. There are also hints as to why these groups may have had plenty to sell when collectors arrived: "No matter how old and worn a utensil, it is rarely destroyed or deliberately thrown out; and an accumulation of property in good, poor, mediocre, and practically worthless condition cumbers most houses" (Kroeber 1925:79). Among the spoons in the Hearst Museum collections are several that have been lovingly repaired with string or hide.

Although Klamath River carving is frequently included in continental surveys of Native American art (for instance, Conn 1979: 268–71), there have been no comprehensive reviews of the subject since Kelly. Virtually the entire collection was on display when the Museum was in San Francisco (between 1903 and 1931, officially opened to the public in 1911), but since moving back to Berkeley, very little of it, especially the larger pieces, has been exhibited. To the best of our knowledge, this is the first exhibition to focus on the carving of the Klamath River region.

PRINCIPAL FORMS AND FUNCTIONS

In his summary of Yurok culture, Alfred Kroeber commented on the "fairly rich civilization" possessed by the Yurok and their neighbors: "In addition to the many sorts of baskets and a considerable number of dance paraphernalia, nearly 100 different kinds of implements of Yurok manufacture have been preserved in museums. Adding those which went out of use before they could be collected, it is safe to say that the group made at least 150, and perhaps 200, distinct types of utensils" (1925:97). An important number of these objects were carved. These objects range greatly in size and scale from tiny, finely worked pipes and spoons to seventeen-foot redwood canoes. "Carving," however, is a Eurocentric concept; any relation to a Native category has not yet been determined. The grouping employed here is merely for our convenience, as carving has been defined in the dominant culture. Many of the objects covered in the exhibition and publication were, in fact, produced by abrading, pecking, or grinding, and not carving—cutting away with a knife. Nevertheless, these alternative techniques had much the same result: a shaped hard material, quite distinctive in effect from the fabrication of hides, feathers, or plant fibers (the other principal Klamath River materials). All the forms considered here can be characterized as a sculptural tradition, broadly defined. This essay attempts to review the full range of Klamath River carving in all forms and media, from the turn of the century to the present.[5]

Isabel Kelly's monograph dealt with three major varieties of decorated carving: elk antler spoons, wooden paddles for stirring acorn mush, and elk antler containers (called purses) for dentalium shell money. She also considered wooden chests (cylindrical boxes) for the storage of valuables, and other incised articles (hairpins, combs, net gauges, dentalium shell money). Our exhibit/publication also includes objects without incised designs which, nevertheless, often possess beautifully shaped forms: house parts (roof and wall planks, carved doors), house ladders, headrests, stools, canoes, miniature canoes, netting shuttles, fishing clubs, food platters and trays, and pipes.

Houses. Perhaps the master container in a culture deeply concerned with the storage of valuables is the house.[6] While most of the house was not carved per se, the same kinds of woodworking tools and techniques were used, and the house did contain carved forms such as the doorway, ladders, pillows, and stools. Although the format and use of the region's architecture varied slightly from group to group, the Yurok village was typical—an average of nine dwellings (ranging from three to seventeen) and three sweathouses (Kroeber 1925:82). Like the Hupa house, the dwelling was the "home of the family, the sleeping place of the women, and the storehouse for the family possessions" (Goddard 1903:13). The sweathouses, on the other hand, were used exclusively by the men and older boys for sweating, working, socializing, and sleeping. Yurok houses (or, more precisely, the house sites) were named.

The dwelling was constructed of large planks which formed the

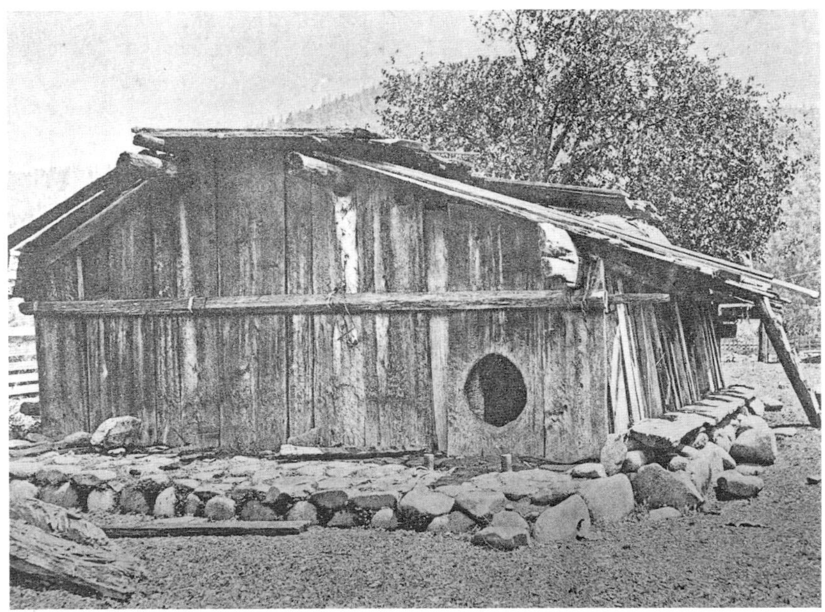

Exterior of a Hupa house.
Photograph by W. C. Blasdale, before 1903 (print no. 13–1339).

walls and roof. These planks were carefully shaped to fit together and shed rain. Generally square to rectangular, the house measured about twenty feet on a side, about six to eight feet high at the peak and about four feet at the eaves. The Hupa and Yurok versions were covered with a three-pitched roof, creating two slanting slides and a flat part on top. Inside, the floor was a pit, three to five feet deep, lined with planks, with the hearth at its center. Surrounding the pit was an earthen ledge, used for storage of the household's possessions. The house was entered through a round doorway placed at one of the frontal corners. A notched log or plank served as a ladder down into the pit. Tolowa houses varied slightly in format from Yurok, Hupa, and Karuk examples (Gould 1978:130–31). Yurok houses were redwood, while Hupa and Karuk houses were built of cedar planks (Goddard 1903:13–18, Bright 1978:183).

Smaller than the dwelling (measuring about twelve feet long, nine to eleven feet across, and six to seven feet high), the sweathouse was built entirely around a pit, with only the pitched roof visible above the ground. An old canoe was often recycled as a ridge cover. The building was entered through a roundish, horizontal opening in the roof. As in the house, a ladder led down into the pit. Unlike the dwelling, the sweathouse typically had an additional exit doorway at the back. These were quite small, some no bigger than fourteen by ten inches, and closed with a snugly fitted wooden plug. They seem too small for the average person to fit through, but Kroeber assures us that they were "habitually used by a little company of varied sizes, as well as their guests. But the bodies are all naked, of course, and supple with perspiration" (1925:81). In contrast to all the possessions in a dwelling house, the interior was usually kept almost bare. Most of these groups also erected sacred sweathouses for ritual use. Every six years, the Yurok, for example, erected an earthly version of a structure that stood at the center of the cosmos (Nabokov and Easton 1989:288, 292).

Beyond the simple splitting and adzing of the roof and wall planks, woodworking for the house included two carved items—doors and ladders. The doorway was a circular hole, about two feet wide, carved into a broad, thick plank, usually the second from the right as one faced the building. Occasionally the door plank was decorated with geometric designs, such as a circle of dots or a chevron. The door itself was a smaller plank that slid in a groove, often the gunwale of an old canoe, held upright by two stakes (Kroeber 1925:78–79). Out of thirty-plus Yurok houses standing in 1902, Kroeber counted eleven carved house doors (1960:164). The principal house ladder, essentially a notched log up to two feet wide, led from the ground level into the pit. Sometimes a second ladder stood at the opposite end for convenience in getting up to the earthen shelf (Kroeber 1960:164–65).

Inside these structures were the household furniture. In their houses, wealthier families had several stools—a flaring, round block, measuring three to nine inches high and about twelve to sixteen inches in diameter. The shorter variety was kept permanently in the sacred houses used in the world renewal ceremonies (Kroeber 1960:165). The pillow or headrest was a simple, yet elegant form—a rectangular block with a scooped-out semicircle. Both objects were associated with men, particularly the pillow, which was kept in the sweathouse.

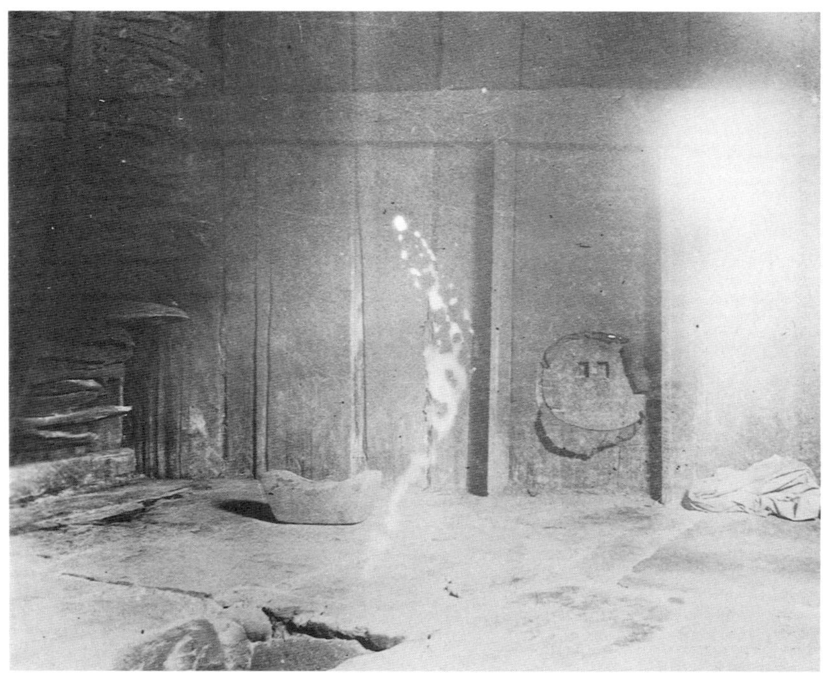

Interior of a Yurok sweathouse. Note the carved door and pillow.
Photograph by Alfred Kroeber, July, 1906 (neg. no. 15–2733).

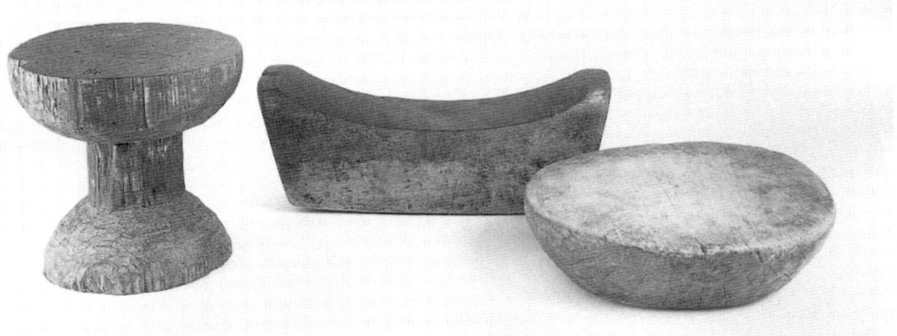

Yurok stool; redwood, 8⅝ in. (22.0 cm.) high, 8¾ in. (22.2 cm.) diameter (1–1867); collected by Alfred L. Kroeber in 1902.

Hupa sweathouse pillow; cedar, 15½ in. (39.4 cm.) long, 5½ in. (14.0 cm.) high, 4¼ in. (10.7 cm.) wide (1–944); collected by Philip M. Jones in 1901.

Yurok stool; redwood, 3½ in. (8.9 cm.) high, 12¼ in. (31.1 cm.) diameter (1–9434); collected by Alfred L. Kroeber in Weitchpec in 1906.

Men reclined on the pillows in order to breathe in the fresh air found near the floor of the smoke-filled structure (Barrett et al. ms.).

Transportation (canoes). As the Native people of Northwest California lived along the rivers and ocean, canoes were the principal mode of transportation.[7] Dugout canoes were used for fishing and travel, and they also played a role in the annual world renewal dances (Kroeber 1925:60–61). Because they were made only of redwood, which was restricted to the coast, canoes were produced only by the Yurok, Tolowa, and Wiyot and traded to the upriver Hupa and Karuk. Although their length varied, the dimensions seem to have been standardized at about eighteen feet long, three to four feet wide, and ten to twenty inches deep. A canoe of this size could carry about five or six adults. In addition to the usual riverine version, Tolowa and coastal Yurok made large seagoing dugout canoes, thirty to forty feet long and five to ten feet in beam. The Yurok used them for coastal trading, while the Tolowa depended on them for sea-lion hunting. Whereas most adult men owned a river canoe, only the leading men in each village could own a large canoe (Gould 1968).[8]

The simple grace of the coastal canoe is evident. At the ends, the canoe's prow and stern are essentially the same—blunt and curved up about a foot from the sides. This arched shape is best suited for riverine travel, making the craft very maneuverable. The canoe is propelled by a paddle, about six to eight feet long, with a heavy blade at the bottom, held standing up. The seated helmsman used a shorter and broader paddle. When not in use for extended periods, canoes were drawn out of the water and covered from the sun.

The canoe was, and still is, considered a living being, and various interior projections are likened to parts of a body. More common in former times was a separate, carved ornament (the headdress) on the prow of a wealthy man's canoe. Projecting into the canoe from the prow (the ears) is a kind of hook or handle (the nose). Passing through two holes (the eyes) at the sides of the prow is a loop of grapevine or hazel (the necklace) used to secure a towing rope. Along the sides are elegantly in-turned gunwales, which help to strengthen the canoe. A pair of incised lines leads from the nose toward the stern (the lungs or

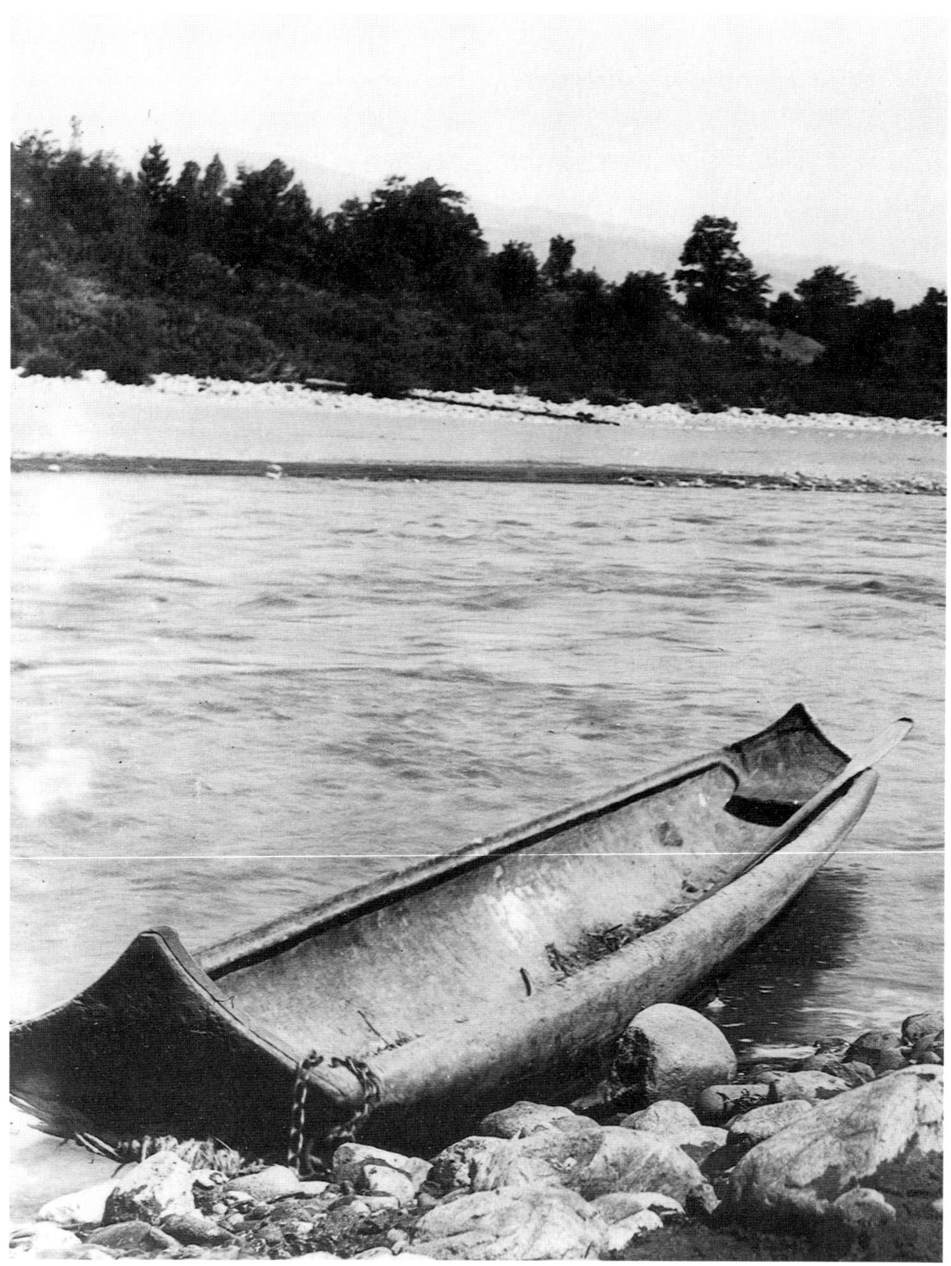

Dugout canoe moored to the shore of the Trinity River at Hostler Ranch.
Photograph by Pliny E. Goddard, 1902 (neg. no. 15–3342).

lifeline). The seat is carved as a jutting projection in the stern. In front of the seat are two footrests (the kidneys, also called by the same Yurok word as ladder-treads; the Hupa called them nipples). In the center bottom of the canoe (the belly) is a rounded knob (the heart). Of no known use in earlier times, by the late nineteenth century it was used as an attachment for a mast. Finally, the paddles were called the boat's "legs" (Spott 1939).

Hunting and Fishing. Men of the Klamath River region employed a few carved forms in their hunting and fishing (Kroeber 1925:84–85). Although the sinew-backed bow played a key role in hunting, it was only minimally carved (Kroeber 1925:89–90, 1960:87–91; Ortiz 1995:30–33). Nevertheless, bows were carved thinly and exactingly, invariably out of yew wood. Fishing involved a greater variety of carved forms, including fish hooks, shuttles (made of wood) and net-mesh measurers (of elk antler) for making fishing nets, net floaters and sinkers, fish clubs, and fish egg mashers (Kroeber and Barrett 1960). Harpoon heads and fish hooks, only slightly carved, were less important in this area than weirs and nets. One group of carved items that were critical were the net making implements (Kroeber and Barrett 1960:60–65). The cord used to make a net was wound around a shuttle, a long stick with a fork at each end, formerly of elk antler and then replaced by a hard wood when iron tools made it easier to carve. The spacing of the net mesh was determined by the net gauge or measure, a thin, flared rectangle (most commonly of antler, but also of bone or wood). These came in several shapes and sizes, depending on the desired kind of net, each suited for a different kind of fish. Net floaters were simple pieces of light wood, while sinkers were often elegantly carved pieces of heavy stone such as serpentine (Kroeber and Barrett 1960:55). Clubs were used to dispatch the fish before removing them from the net (Goddard 1903:23–24). According to Kroeber, "Fish clubs were strictly utilitarian, of wood, sometimes gnarled, never decoratively carved" (1960:83). Often made of redwood or other soft wood, they were usually carved plainly because they were so likely to fall into the river. Similar in form were the mashers, of a harder wood, for berries and fish eggs (especially of the sturgeon), which had to be crushed before curing (Kroeber and Barrett 1960:91).

Food Preparation and Serving. Two of the most varied and elaborate kinds of Klamath River carving were used in food preparation and serving—the mush paddle and the elk antler spoon. Women generally employed basketry rather than carved objects in their gathering and processing of acorns and other foods. The prominent exception was the mush paddle.[9] Women used a wooden paddle to stir the mixture of ground acorn meal and water, which was cooked with hot rocks placed into a large basket (Kroeber 1960:134). "The Yurok paddle is of madroña, manzanita, oak, or other hard wood, and sometimes nearly 4 feet long and quite unwieldy for a seated woman" (Kroeber 1925:87). The paddles used to cook the larger quantities of acorn soup needed for feasts tended to be longer than those used for family meals. Unlike the comparatively small and simple mush paddles of central California, the handles of Klamath River examples were elaborately carved in geometric, often cut-out, patterns.

Acorn mush was eaten with a variety of spoons. Men used finely carved spoons of elk antler (Kroeber 1925:93, 1960:135). The bowl was typically rather large—three by two and one-half inches, holding about two tablespoons. The spoon was held in the left hand, with modest sips taken from the rim (Mason 1889:218). The handles, about three to five inches long, were carved in geometric designs, often heavily incised. Sometimes these were made of wood or bark, but as Kroeber noted, "substandard materials are disliked" (1960:135). The gender-distinction of Klamath River society is marked by the restriction of women to spoons of mussel shell or part of an animal skull (often a deer). Even here, a certain cultural style prevailed, for these were often polished and stained. Rich men kept large sets of elk antler spoons in order to serve their guests at feasts; one Yurok man (Long Charlie of Murek) owned fifteen to twenty as part of his personal wealth (Kroeber 1976:353). Spoons were stored in openwork baskets (O'Neale 1932:34).[10]

While basketry supplied the bulk of the region's food containers,

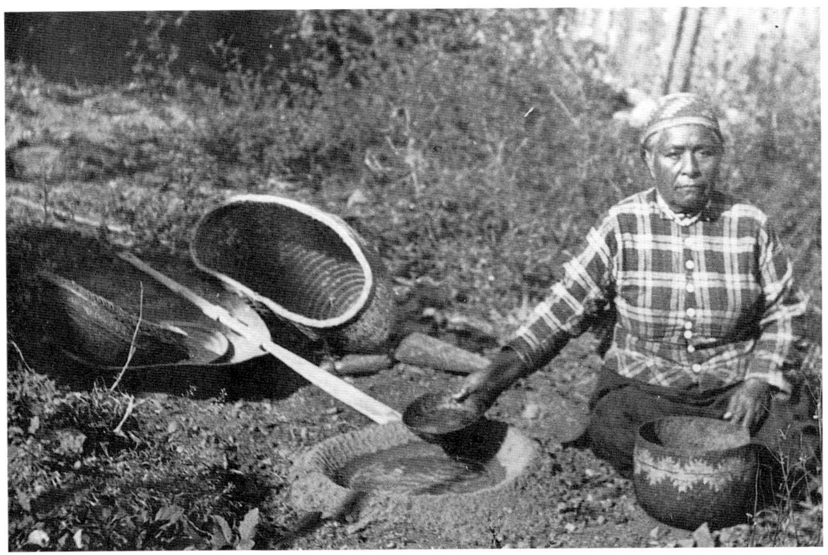

Mary (Karuk) leaching acorns, with a mush paddle at her side.
Photograph probably by John Daggett (print no. 13–2432).

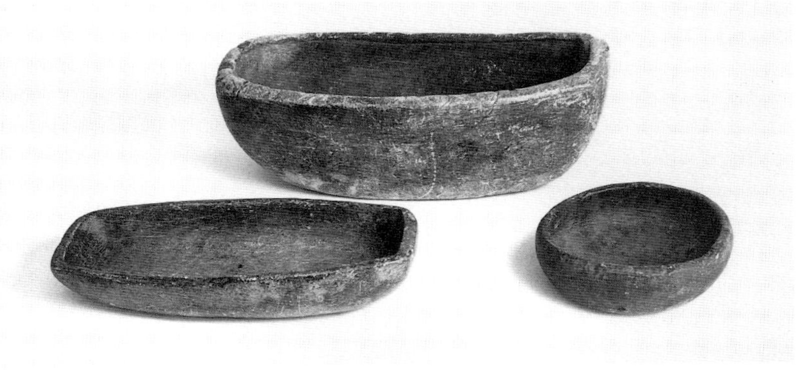

Steatite stone bowls for catching fish oil.

Yurok; 13½ in. (34.2 cm.) long, 6¼ in. (15.8 cm.) wide, 2½ in. (6.4 cm.) high; collected by Philip M. Jones in 1901 (1–1020).

Yurok; 16¾ in. (42.5 cm.) long, 10 in. (25.4 cm.) wide, 5¾ in. (14.5 cm.) high; collected by Alfred L. Kroeber in Orick in 1906 (1–9391).

Tolowa; 7⅛ in. (18.0 cm.) diameter, 2⅛ in. (5.5 cm.) high; collected by Pliny E. Goddard in Crescent City in 1902 (1–2514).

there were several kinds of platters and bowls (Kroeber 1925:92). Rough rectangular platters of redwood or cedar were used only for deer meat (Kroeber 1960:136).[11] The Hupa and Yurok used wooden bowls for washing the fingers following the eating of venison, ensuring that no particle of the animal would remain in the house (Goddard 1903:23, Kroeber 1960:138). Shallow steatite bowls and platters were made for collecting dripping deer or fish grease, but not for serving or eating food (Goddard 1903:26, Kroeber 1960:136). Larger, deeper steatite bowls were used to store fish oil. Set into holes in the house floor, they were covered with a basketry lid (Kroeber and Barrett 1960:103).

Personal Adornment. While clothing was generally formed of fiber and hide, with shell and seeds when decorated, a few carved objects played a part in the care of the body. Small hairpins were made of bone. A flattened spatula of wood, bone, or elk antler seems to have had several functions. A girl at puberty used one as a comb when observing the taboo against scratching herself with her fingers (Kroeber 1925:45, Thompson 1916:46). Men also employed a version—longer than a woman's—when combing the hair for ritual occasions (Thompson 1916:151–52), and when used in pairs, they served as crushers of hair lice (Frank 1900:76). When in the sweathouse, men used a similar device of bone or antler to scrape off sweat.

Valuables and Their Storage. As these cultures were marked by gradations of status and wealth, it is not surprising that carving played an important role in the storage of valuables. There were four principal kinds of Yurok wealth. Most similar to money in function were the dentalium shells (Kroeber 1925:22–25, 1960:215–17), "graded into standardized denominations of value according to intact length, and in terms of which almost anything else could be appraised" (Kroeber 1960:212). Dentalium is a tubular white shell that the Klamath River Indians obtained mostly by trade from the north, particularly off the coast of Vancouver Island. Smaller shells were used for decoration, but the currency-grade shell, "real" money, was often carved with shallow incising, rubbed with pigment, and wrapped with snake skin and woodpecker feathers (Mason 1889:232). The other main forms of wealth were red woodpecker scalps, regalia made of furs, skins (especially white deerskins) and feathers, and large obsidian blades (Kroeber 1960:212–18). As "broken obsidian blades and broken dentalia lost nearly all their value" (Kroeber 1960:215), containers were important.

Dentalium shell money was stored in elk antler purses (Kroeber 1925:93). Measuring about six or seven inches long, they came in several formats, most commonly a longitudinal piece of antler, resting horizontally. The hollowed central cavity formed a receptacle for repeatedly folded strings of dentalium money. Sometimes, the tail of some furry animal would be placed inside the cavity to keep the money from rattling around (Mason 1889:231). A long, narrow antler lid covered the opening, often held in place by an overhanging projection and secured with a hide thong. Many purses in museums have lost their lids. A less typical kind of purse was upright in orientation, resting on a fork formed by the branching tines of the antler. More rarely, purses were also made from the smaller deer antlers. Although some were left plain, the surfaces of purses were usually covered with incised geometric designs. Purses "might be stowed in small, spherical baskets, set in turn into larger ones or into near-cylindrical redwood trunks" (Kroeber 1960:218).

The Yurok, in particular, had large redwood chests in which they stored large items of regalia such as hide costumes, featherwork, or large obsidian blades (Kroeber 1925:92). They were a hollowed-out tapering cylinder (less often rectangular), about two to four feet long, with a lashed-on lid. Although Kroeber saw a relation with canoes, their shape bears a striking resemblance to the elk antler purses. And like the purses, their ends were often decorated with parallel encircling ridges (which helped keep the straps from falling off [Kroeber 1960:218]). These chests could be carried with a strap or transported in the bottom of a canoe. Along with the purses, the chests and the wealth they contained were stored in the "great houses," the homes of Klamath River aristocrats. "From about 1910 on," noted Kroeber, "the Yurok began to like American suit cases for storage of their treasures and for transport of them to dances" (1960:218). Today,

Klamath River people often use old-fashioned, hard-sided suitcases, or even footlockers if they have a lot of regalia.

Ceremonial/Miscellaneous. Carving played a relatively minor part in Klamath River ceremonialism, which was expressed materially more in feathered and hide regalia. One somewhat "religious" carved object was the tobacco pipe (Kroeber 1925:88–89; 1960:224, 245–47; Harrington 1932:135–73). Among the Hupa, smoking was primarily for male relaxation, especially in the sweathouse, while the Yurok associated it with "purification, the supernatural world, and serious ends" (Kroeber 1960:224). Tobacco, the standard offering to the gods, was the only plant cultivated by the Yurok and their neighbors. Generally adult men smoked, women only if they were doctors; people smoked lying down.

Pipes were typically made of hardwood with an inlaid soapstone bowl, but versions of all-wood and all-stone were also common.[12] Those owned by poorer people were all wood. Sometimes pipe bowls and stems were decorated with abalone inserts. The pipe flared at both ends, more so at the bowl. Its size varied, from about three to twelve inches, with the average about six. Doctors' pipes and "show pieces" were especially long (Kroeber 1925:88). Pipes for ceremonial use sometimes came in matched pairs (Ortiz 1994:20). Pipes were stored in hide pouches, a custom restricted in California to the northwestern groups (Kroeber 1925:89).

Among the miscellaneous carved objects were miniature canoes, made as curios for sale or as children's toys (Kroeber 1960:226). Tiny versions are hung from the cradle baskets of baby boys. Contemporary carver Frank Gist has made miniature canoes that are burned after a death. This may be a reference to the Yurok belief that the dead use a canoe to travel across a river to the underworld (Kroeber 1925:47). Gist says it is so "the spirit can go on and continue."

Finally, there is some indication that Klamath River peoples had a form of figurative sculpture (Pilling 1978:150).[13] In the 1870s, Powers reported a redwood human figurine, which he interpreted as some kind of fishing spirit. He also cited the reports of A. W. Chase who said similar figures were erected in commemoration of killing the enemy in battle (Powers 1877:57–58). Disputing Powers' fishing interpretation, Kroeber argued that the figure was more likely to have been a battle trophy (1960:456).

There was a definite technological and artistic style to the region's carving. As Kroeber noted, most Klamath River arts "were carried to a distinctive pitch" (1925:1). Northwestern peoples had several kinds of unique objects such as the stool, pillow, purse, and storage chest; they tended to prefer more laborious materials; and they often made objects in standard sizes and weights (Kroeber 1960:173, 177). In addition to the elaborate designs on so many of their carved pieces, one often finds a stark, geometric clarity. Although it is hard to define this regional style precisely, anyone with a little familiarity with Native California artifacts soon learns to pick out Klamath River objects in a gallery or museum storeroom.

THE ROLE OF THE CARVER

Unfortunately, there is little direct evidence concerning the training, compensation, and social role of carvers in Klamath River societies at the turn of the century. Despite this, the ethnographic literature offers us enough general information to form a fairly accurate picture.

Most fundamental, perhaps, is the pervasive gender specialization of these societies. It seems that the production of carved objects was restricted to males. Men made all the hunting weapons and equipment and did all the wood working, including house and canoe construction (Kroeber 1960:397). They also made all the fine fur and featherwork for regalia. Even the use of carving was gender-related. Most of the carved items seemed to have been used by men—canoes, bows, antler spoons, and purses. Only men could use the elk antler spoons and the stools in the sweathouses. The principal carved form that women used were the mush paddles; other objects were hair combs and pipes.

Although Yurok society was marked by degrees of rank and wealth, professional occupations were not very specialized (Kroeber 1960:396–401). According to Kroeber, there were neither full-time

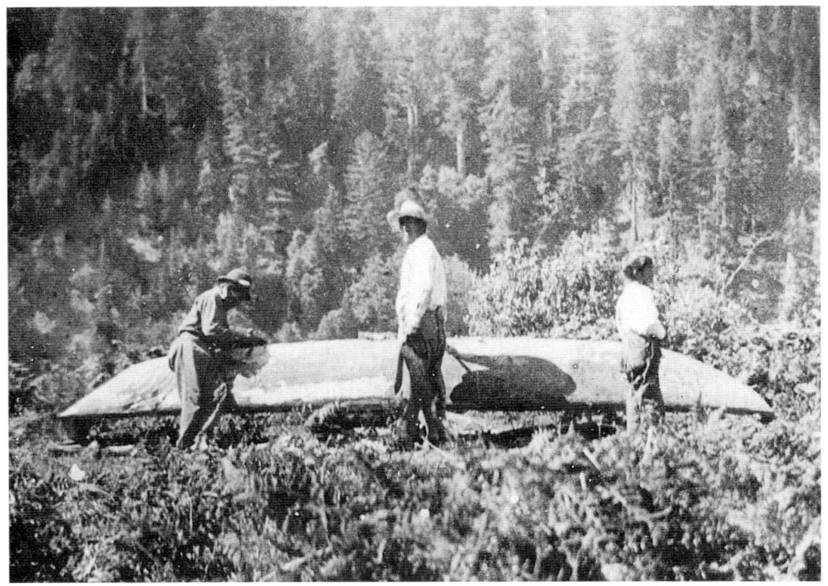

Yurok men working on an unfinished canoe.
Photograph by Mary Dickson (print no. 13–203).

specialists, nor organized groups of specialists. The closest were curing shamans. "There were men who specialized in obsidian chipping, canoe building, net weaving, feather gluing, tobacco growing: not to the point of principal livelihood, but so that they were known for superior skill and predilection and their product was purchased, or their ability hired" (1960:398). Even these men, who excelled at some task, also did the normal chores of a man, such as fishing or hunting.[14]

One fascinating exception to this commonality of skills was in the case of people with a physical disability: "Labor requiring patience as well as manual dexterity (assembly of regalia, rubbing elkhorn spoons into shape, etc.) was often performed by men with crippled backs or legs" (Kroeber 1960:398). A case in point was William Johnson of Rekwoi (Requa), who may have been Kroeber's informant for elk antler spoon-making. According to Kroeber (1976:437), Johnson was crippled from sickness. "However, he was skillful with his hands and specialized in making woodpecker bands, whence he was called Rekwoi eskerwits. *Skerwits* means craftsman, or fine work. It is used also of a woman who makes fine designs on her baskets." One Karuk consultant reported that steatite dishes were "dug out" of stone blocks "by older people unable to engage in more active pursuits; for instance, by an old woman who could no longer make baskets" (Kroeber and Barrett 1960:103).

With regard to media, again we have little direct evidence. Did carvers work equally in wood, antler, and stone, or did they concentrate on a single medium? Given the generality of skills among Klamath River peoples, the average man probably did work in all media, allowing individuals to excel in certain media and forms as their talents dictated. It is clear that general tool use could be applied across materials.

The role of Klamath River aristocrats in carving is also unclear. Anthropologist Arnold Pilling has estimated that aristocrats were about 5 percent of the Yurok population and 10 percent of the males (1978:142). We do know that as part of their upbringing, boys from "high families" were taught to make a set of bow, arrows, and arrowheads, and aristocratic men were certainly the ceremonial leaders. The high-born priests of the great houses, who did not marry, often spent their time making regalia. "Formerly, a few rich men manufactured regalia as a part-time specialty, although it may have been primarily for display of their own wealth" (Pilling 1978:148). Although we have no indication that carving was part of their expertise, one recent aristocratic regalia-maker, Dewey George, was a carver (Pilling 1989:431–32).

Most likely, Klamath River carving was produced by those who were good at it. Given the development of a money economy, the aristocrats probably hired and paid them to produce prestige items like elk antler spoons. For large items like houses and canoes, wealthy men were responsible for feeding the work crew, generally consisting of their close male relatives (Barrett et al. ms.:41; Gould 1968:17–18). Speaking generally of Yurok objects, Pilling noted, "Once produced, such an item could be claimed by its producer, sold to or inherited by another person or descent group, passed into general use in the culture, or placed permanently under taboo at the death of the creator" (1978:146). Although we shall probably never know exactly how, carved items may have been subject to all of these actions.

MATERIALS, TOOLS, AND TECHNIQUES

Although we have little evidence on turn-of-the-century carving practice, the ethnographic literature allows us to form a general picture, which contemporary carvers can greatly supplement. Wood was perhaps the most common material carved by Klamath River peoples, but elk antler seems to have been the more prestigious medium; stone implements were also common. Taken together, these hard materials formed a cultural complex apart from women's crafts—most notably basketry—made of plant fibers.

For the coastal peoples, redwood was the favored type of wood, employed in houses and furniture (stools, pillows, trunks) and for canoes and paddles. This wood, the substance for the largest and most important items in Yurok culture, was more than an inert material. It was a spiritual entity, personified as a character in Yurok myths as one of the *wogey* or primordial beings (Kroeber 1976:394). Captain Spott of Requa narrated a fascinating story of the origin of redwood and its use for boats:

> Sky-Owner, Pulekukwerek, and Wohpekumeu [the culture hero/trickster] did not know how the river would be crossed. Pulekukwerek said, "What shall we do that persons may cross? How will they live? I do not know." Wohpekumeu did not know. They had no wood. Then suddenly someone grew up quickly there. He said, "That is what I came for. I can be used for boats. They will make boats of me and cross the river." Pulekukwerek said, "What is your name?" He said, "Do you not know my name? Pulekukwerek said, "No, but I would like to know." He said, "I am called Redwood." Pulekukwerek said, "It is good that you grew so quickly. Now persons will live (properly)." Redwood said, "I want them to put pitch on my head. I want them also to put pitch on my stern, and I want a withe around my neck. That is the way I like it." Then Pulekukwerek told him, "Yes, that is good. That is how they will use you." (Kroeber 1976:427–28).

The myth accounts for redwood's rapid growth rate as well as the need for pitch and withe reinforcements on the canoe ends. Canoes were made from one half of a log, with the bottom made out of the inner, denser heartwood. As the cross-grain ends were the weakest part, they were often covered with pitch and reinforced with lashings. After contact, they were reinforced along the top with metal strips.

As redwood grows only along the coast, the Hupa and Karuk used cedar for their houses and most of their wooden items—house furniture like ladders, trunks, pillows, chests, platters, stools—and purchased redwood canoes from the Yurok. They were able to choose from the three kinds of cedar that grow in Northwest California: canoe or Western red cedar *(Thuja)*, Incense cedar *(Libocedrus)*, and Port Orford cedar *(Chamaecyparis)* (Kroeber 1960:179–80). Hardwoods such as madrone, manzanita, yew, and maple were used for pipes, paddles, and spoons (on the identities and uses of woods among the Karuk, see Schenck and Gifford 1952).

The hard, white elk antlers were used for purses and spoons, as well as net gauges, net shuttles, and combs. Although the region's Native peoples hunted elk, it was not necessary to kill the animal in order to obtain the antlers. Elk antler is an annually renewable resource. Grown only by the male, each spring the elk drops its antlers in order grow a new pair (Petersen 1988:41). We do know that among the Yurok, families owned the rights to gather shed elk antler on specified tracts of land (Pilling 1978:147). One of the factors that may have curtailed the production of elk antler spoons and purses was the almost complete extinction of the elk in the Klamath River area around the turn of the century. Kroeber argues that wooden spoons were made in imitation of the elk antler kind, "devised when the supply of antler was no longer obtainable" (1925:93).

Elk antler was the prestige material, with wood definitely a less desirable substitution. "The Yurok take very little account of wedges, spoons, mesh measures, etc. made in wood: elk antler was standard, and inferior material was avoided, perhaps just because it was easier to work" (Kroeber 1960:177). The antlers of elk were preferred to those of deer because they were both larger and softer. Kroeber and Barrett speculate that sharp-edged metal tools allowed the carving of wood. "Any wooden shuttle in precontact days was probably used by a poor man who could not afford better material and whose whole equipment was substandard" (1960:60). Similarly, the rare wood net measures "were either temporary implements or were used by lower-class or shiftless men and were usually referred to as a 'poor man's mesh measure' " (Kroeber and Barrett 1960:61).

A mythic perspective on these materials and methods was shared with Kroeber in 1902 by the Karuk Sweet William of Ishipishi. In addition to fish spears, flint knives, acorn-cooking rocks, bows and arrows, Fish Hawk (or Osprey) was the inventor of spoons.

> Now they had no spoons. Fish Hawk thought, "How can they eat acorns without a spoon? I will make a spoon of leaves." Then he made it of that. "I do not think it is the right way, the way I have made the spoon. It will not last long. I will make it of wood. I think it will be better." Then he thought, "How shall I make it? I will make it with mussel shell." Then he used mussel shell to cut it with, and made a spoon of wood. Then he thought, "I do not think it is right. That spoon will break easily. Many elk grow on the hills: I will make a spoon of elkhorn. I think it will be better." Then he went on the hill looking for elk antlers. He thought, "I think somewhere I will find horns that have been dropped by elk; from them I can make spoons." He found antlers and brought them down. "Now I will make a spoon. That is the kind to use. That is the kind to make a spoon from with mussel shell." Then the mussel shell broke every little while, and he thought, "Let me make it with white rock." He saw white rock (quartzite) outdoors and cracked some of it: it was very sharp. Then he began to work with it. Now he made the elk horn spoon right and it was good. Then elkhorn spoons were to be seen: that is why human beings now make them" (Kroeber and Gifford 1980:73).

Despite a few vague comments in the literature (Kelly 1930b:344), there seems to be no firsthand report of how elk antler was carved in the nineteenth century. From Kelly's comment (citing a conversation with Yurok Robert Johnson), we may conclude that Kroeber himself seems never to have observed this. In 1960 Samuel Barrett filmed Yurok Homer Cooper making a spoon of elk antler, using only stone for cutting and polishing, but there is evidence that Cooper had never done this before and was following Barrett's instructions (Barrett 1961a). Although carvers now use machine tools, our best idea of elk antler carving comes from contemporary artists like George Blake and Frank Gist.

Carvers of Northwest California became expert in understanding and exploiting the strengths and weaknesses of elk antler as an artistic medium. Each antler has a soft, spongy core—essentially the marrow—where the blood vessels once were, covered by the hard, white outer surface. This combination of soft interior and hard exterior is perfectly suited for making a container out of the hollowed central cavity. This structure does present problems, however, for making a spoon, as the spongy core would not be impervious to liquids. The artists were thus careful to select just that part of the antler that could be formed into a hard spoon—the wide base and the side—with all the rest being cut away. Because of this physical limitation, a spoon can only be made from one part of each antler—the base. While the rest can be made into purses, combs, or net gauges, there is only one spoon per antler. Frank Gist estimated that from one fairly large antler, he could probably make four to five large purses, several smaller purses, as well as the single spoon.[15]

The shape of the elk antler tends to be more constraining than is the case with wood. Before beginning work, the artist has to "study" the piece. As Gist said, "When I look at a horn, I see where I'm going to make my spoons, where I'm going to make my purses. I look at the horn for its potential, for what type of spoon I can get out of it." These spatial constraints carry over to the level of design, as well: "The shape of the horn dictates what type of design it will have. I look at where my handle is going to be, what kind of design I can get out of it, how wide it is going to be, how long of a handle do I have." In applying incised designs to purses, for example, carvers say that they have to adapt the design to the shape and format of the antler; not every design will work on every antler.

Kelly notes that in the old days antler spoons were steamed and cut into shape (1930b:344), perhaps like Northwest Coast mountain sheep and goat spoons, but there is little evidence for this statement. In later years, Kroeber denied that spoons were steamed, "the dry

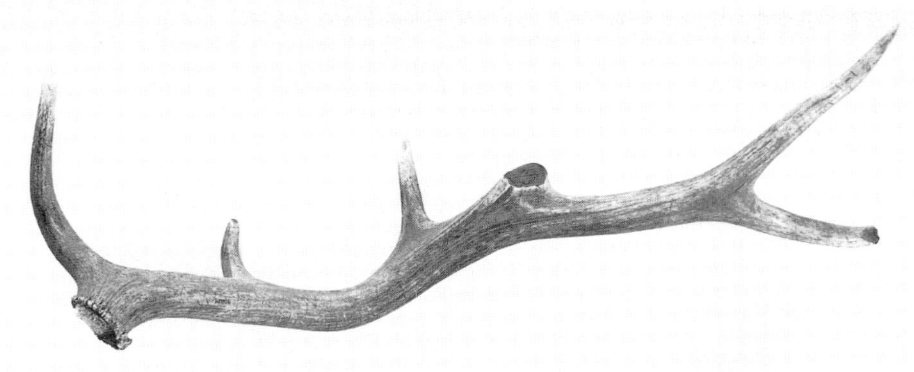

Stages in making an elk antler spoon: natural antler. 30½ in. (77.5 cm.) from base to tip; collected by Samuel A. Barrett, pre-1965 (1–259061).

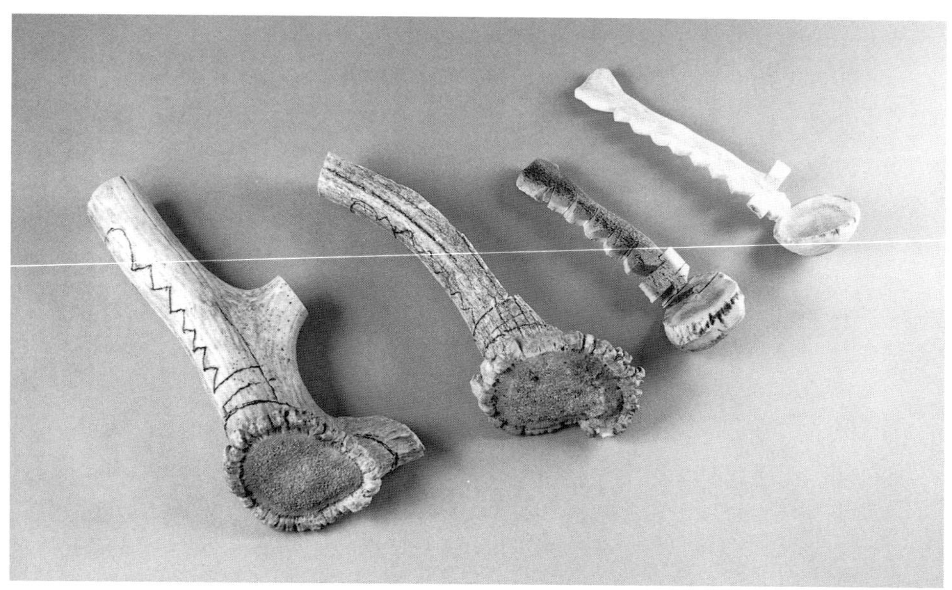

Stages in making an elk antler spoon: four steps by Frank Gist, 1995. *Left to right:* 8½ in. (21.6 cm) long (1–259293). 8½ in. (21.6 cm.) long (1–259294). 6¾ in. (17.2 cm.) long (1–259295). 7¾ in. (19.7 cm.) long (1–259296). Gist shapes the spoon with a band saw and rotary grinder. The designs in the first two stages were added for display purposes, to show the orientation of the final shape.

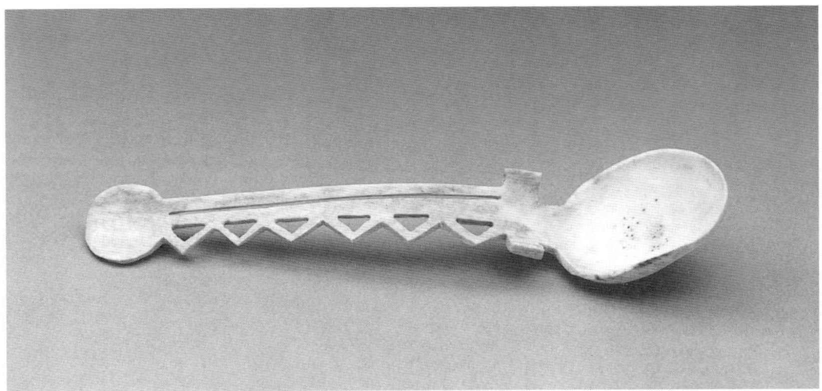

Stages in making an elk antler spoon: finished spoon by Frank Gist, 1995; 7⅛ in. (18.2 cm.) long (1–259278). This is Gist's version of a Yurok spoon (1–1943) illustrated in Isabel Kelly (plate 106-h).

horn could probably be shaped better by abrading than by scraping with flint" (1960:135).[16] In the pre-contact period, both spoons and wooden pipes were shaped roughly with a flint or obsidian knife, then abraded with a rock such as sandstone, and finished by a smoothing with horsetail rushes (Thompson 1916:35, Kroeber 1960:135). Although the pipes seem so perfectly even that they must have been made on a lathe (as Otis Mason thought, 1889:220), they were all hand-carved. In later times, some Karuk used glass bottle fragments for shaping manzanita wood spoons and pipes (Harrington 1932:149–50).

With time, elk antler acquires a warm, brown patina as it is handled and used (Kroeber and Barrett 1960:61). The old spoons in museum collections are invariably a deep, dark chocolate color, obtained as the spoons were repeatedly dipped into the tannic acorn mush. George Blake notes that some yellowing of antler will occur through exposure to the smoke in the house. Compared to elk antler, bone was a relatively minor material in the region. The Tolowa used it to make needles for weaving mats of tule reeds, and the Karuk made bone awls for sewing hides (Bright 1978:183).

Stone also had an important place in Klamath River carving, especially in earlier days. Hard granite or basalt was especially favored for mauls, adz handles, net sinkers, and acorn-pounding pestles. The softer sandstone served for finer work, such as grinding antler. Soapstone or steatite was the favored material for pipe bowls and sometimes entire pipes because it was one of the few stones that could be heated to a high temperature without breaking (Heizer and Elsasser 1980:148). It was also used for the rough stone trays for deer or salmon fat. In addition to arrowheads and large, ceremonial obsidian blades, small flint knives lashed to wooden handles were used for scaling and slitting salmon, and possibly formerly for skinning and cutting deer.

Klamath River carvers often worked to standard dimensions. Yurok canoe-carvers used touch to guide their work: "They gauged [the thickness of the side walls] by placing one hand outside and the other inside, moving both hands slowly along—and it is surprising how even the thickness is in all parts" (Thompson 1916:33). The older Hupa, Goddard noted (1903:50), had "a series of marks tattooed on their legs similar to those on the arms by which money is measured. By means of these the height of the canoe is easily estimated. The width marked on a paddle handle is ascertained by measuring with the extended arms. Nearly all articles were manufactured by reference to the tattooed lines or to some part of the body as a measure."

No work area has been reported for carvers, though they may have performed some of their labor in the sweathouse. "In each village, the adult men and boys from the age of puberty onward lived together in the so-called sweathouse (where sweatbaths were only one of a series of male-oriented activities—gambling, net making, bow making—carried out in this building)" (Gould 1978:131). Given the darkness of sweathouses, however, much of their work was probably performed outdoors. The roof of the sweathouse was used for lounging in good weather (Barrett et al. ms.:45), and "Each coastal village also had a separate detached area devoted to activities like making stone tools, splitting wood, heavy butchering of sea lions, and fish cleaning" (Gould 1978:131).

Tools. While tools such as adzes, axes, and drills were a means to produce other pieces of carving, they were often exquisitely crafted objects in their own right (Kroeber 1925:94–95, Kroeber 1960:

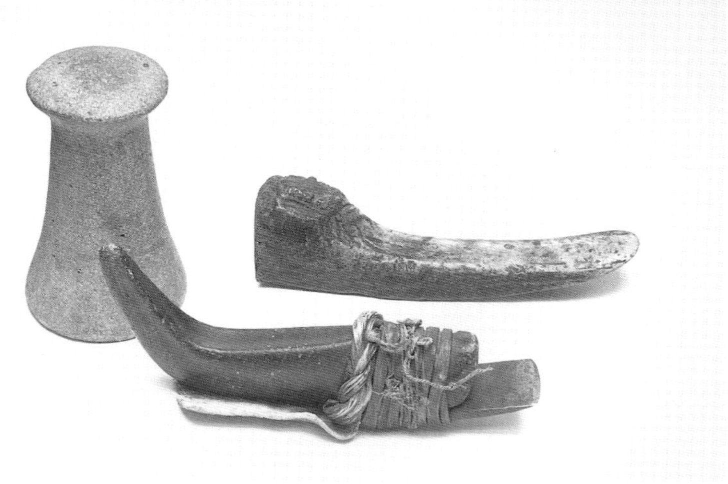

Woodworking tools (Yurok).

Stone maul; 5⅞ in. (14.8 cm.) high, 3⅞ in. (9.7 cm.) diameter at base; collected by Alfred L. Kroeber in Shregon in 1901 (1–11836).

Adz; stone handle, iron blade lashed on with hide strips and twine, rawhide finger protector; 9½ in. (24.2 cm.) long; collected by Philip M. Jones in 1901 (1–1173).

Elk antler wedge; 9½ in. (24.2 cm.) long; collected by Alfred L. Kroeber in 1901 (1–1549).

177–82). Generally, the same tools used for woodworking were also employed for working antler and other materials. Cutting down large redwoods with shell and stone tools was difficult, so these coastal carvers favored logs that had naturally fallen. Otherwise, the logs were burned and chiseled away with wedges and adzes. Rough shaping with fire was employed especially for hollowing out canoes. Planks were split off from the logs with elk antler wedges and stone mauls and then further worked with stone adzes. Except on their house planks, Klamath River carvers generally avoided showing tool marks. They used sandstone for both shaping and rough smoothing. The finishing was accomplished with horsetail rush, commonly called "Indian sandpaper" (Kroeber 1960:179). A final finish was given to canoes by burning chips and shavings over the surface and then rubbing off the charred area.

Elk wedges, from a few inches to about eighteeen inches long, varied in shape, more or less straight or curved depending on the intended task: "Those for starting a split were sharply curved; for developing it, slightly curved; and for just pushing the crack through, as straight as possible" (Kroeber 1960:177). They were given an edge by rubbing on stone, and, according to Thompson (1916:35), given a hard edge by drying before a fire after being rubbed with grease. Lesser versions came in wood. Wedges were also used for cross-cut chiseling. The mauls were six to eight inches of very hard stone—a basalt or "mottled metamorphic stone" (Kroeber 1925:94)—and weighed between two and a half to four pounds. One especially large kind of maul, restricted to one or two per village, had to be used by two men (Kroeber 1960:178). Mauls were usually very symmetrical, with a flat, wide butt, sometimes a rounded head, and were quite highly polished.

Another tool made of stone was the adz. Unlike wooden Northwest coast examples, Klamath River adz handles were made of stone. Six to ten inches long, the handle was curved at the end, forming a **J**. (Sometimes the curved end broke off and was smoothed down as a straight handle). The opposite end was cut away to fit the butt of the blade, which was lashed on. Most pieces have two or three ridges or grooves to hold the lashings, and usually a flat strip of hide to protect the knuckles. Soon after contact, steel tips replaced the heavy blades of mussel shell or stone, but they were hafted to the same stone handles.

Iron may have been more important in "traditional" Klamath River carving than we have yet realized. Kroeber was uncertain "with what the Yurok did their finer wood carving, as on the acorn mush stirrers. Elkhorn spoons had their [handle] designs rubbed into form with sandstone. Purses, of the same material but hollow, must have been gouged with a sharper tool. The method of boring pipes of hard wood and stone is also unascertained" (1925:94). "It seems doubtful whether this type of knife [with a small flint blade] could have been effectually used in woodworking" (1960:179). Kroeber's lack of knowledge became clear as he continued, "The Yurok had no nineteenth-century woodworker's knife of iron or other material. Aboriginally, they may have depended wholly on wedge and adz, plus sandstone for rubbing. Their elkhorn spoons, whose handles are often zigzag and even openwork, were largely shaped by rubbing with sandstone, no doubt after some boring. Unfortunately, the whole matter of the transverse cutting of wood, whether in logs, timbers, or small objects, seems not to have been inquired into."

After contact, these cutting points were quickly replaced with iron. Accounts of the first European contact with the Yurok, a 1775 Spanish visit to a village near Trinidad, already note the presence of iron (Heizer and Mills 1952:24–26). Later, in 1828, Jedediah Smith found Yuroks with beads, knives, and "arrow points of iron" (Pilling 1978:140). "A little iron had drifted in before 1850 in large but thin spearpoint-shaped blades which were used as knives; plus perhaps some pieces of barrel hoop, etc." (Kroeber 1960:178).

Native access to iron increased dramatically after the 1850 gold rush. In their analysis of a Yurok village near Trinidad, Heizer and Mills noted an interesting increase in carved steatite objects after this date. "This increase is due no doubt to the availability of metal-pointed chisels made from files, which are effective implements for working the soft steatite. Similarly, the metal ax, hatchet, and saw made the making of planks much easier, though this effect on the native woodworking complex may have lasted only until sawed lumber from local mills or abandoned houses was available for salvage" (1952:15–16). Powers noted the dramatic effect that iron-tipped blades had on Yurok carvings. Two men would take five to six months to carve a canoe with the old methods of burning, scraping, and rubbing, whereas they could finish the job in several days using their new iron blades (1877:48). A relatively early demise for stoneworking is indicated by Mason's report that while heavy stone mauls "were still used by the old men among the Hupas" in the late nineteenth century, none of them "were able to make one. Those now in possession are much battered, have been handed down for generations, and are highly prized" (1889:208).

Given this evidence, one might hypothesize that most of the Klamath River carvings in museum collections were made with iron-tipped tools, and not the "traditional" sandstone, antler, or shell (see

Kelly 1930b:344–45). Modern carvers like George Blake and Frank Gist freely use machine tools, but such technological innovations are nothing new, and the use of these modern tools does not make the finished product any less "authentic." As Blake responds, "When people come to buy a canoe in a covered wagon, I'll make it with old-time tools" (Ortiz 1990:14).

Finally, there may be a broader regional parallel here between Northwest California and the Northwest Coast. As these more northern groups gained access to traded iron-tipped tools, they were given the means necessary to carve large, free-standing totem poles and intricate, articulated masks. This allowed an artistic efflorescence that has long been seen as "traditional" and "authentic," when it was, in fact, a cultural creative innovation (Blackman 1976). Although it is still only a surmise, the same may be true for California.

AESTHETICS: DESIGNS AND SYMBOLISM

We do not have a detailed understanding of the aesthetic system that guided the creation and appreciation of these beautiful objects. Here we miss sorely a carving counterpart of Lila O'Neale's exhaustive interviews with Klamath River basket weavers (1932). As we can see from Kroeber's remark that "*Skerwits* means craftsman, or fine work. It is used also of a woman who makes fine designs on her baskets" (1976:437), nineteenth century carving also must have been part of such an aesthetic system.

The basic forms of Klamath River carving show a clear cultural style—simple, strong geometric shapes, as seen, for instance, in the plain but elegantly decorated stools or the flaring walls of the canoe. The most elaborate examples of this aesthetic tradition are found in the amazing variety of spoon and mush paddle handles. Exactly why they would be so varied is unclear. The elk antler spoons, of course, would be displayed before guests at a feast, and thus would make an impression of beauty, wealth, and material accumulation. Yet the equally impressive mush paddles would be used and seen principally by the women as they cooked. When asked how and why they choose handle designs, contemporary carvers say that it is their aesthetic choice, based on what appeals to them, and perhaps this was also the case in the past. Not all such objects were decorated, however. Sometimes spoons, paddles, and purses were left plain. These may have been unfinished, intended for everyday use, or owned by poorer people.

One feature of mush paddle design has a functional foundation. In her formal analysis, Kelly examined the decorative protuberances at the top and bottom of the handle, which she called, respectively, the capital and pedestal (1930b:350). Blake and Gist point out that these points, so often elaborated in design, served as functional hand-grips when stirring the acorn mush. It seems clear that, in this case at least, the decoration was stimulated by a functional necessity.

Color plays a relatively minor role in Klamath River carving. Paints were mixtures of a pigment and a binder of fish glue, stored in a small stone bowl (Kroeber and Barrett 1960:104, Jacknis 1991:171). Black, the most common color, was frequently rubbed into the incised lines of elk antler purses. While we are uncertain of its composition, it appears to be similar to the black body and face paint (and tattooing pigment) of charcoal or soot mixed with deer marrow (Kroeber 1960:209). Occasionally red and blue were used, more often on the purse ends. These three are also the principal colors for other painted items like drum heads, sinew-backed bows, and ceremonial hide and fiber items such as deerhide robes, crocheted head nets (commonly called "hangers"), and wolf-skin headbands.[17] In addition to purses, net measurers, sweat-scrapers, and hair pins were also incised.

Klamath River carving—in fact, all their decorative art, including their basketry—is typically rendered in a distinctive style of geometric designs, most often triangles and zigzags. We have little direct evidence on the naming of carving patterns and designs. The most revealing statement is Kroeber's observation that "Basket design names are the only names applied by the Yurok to the carved, engraved, or painted figures, predominatingly of triangles, on wooden acorn-soup paddles, elkhorn spoons and purses, and network and skin" (1905:130).[18] According to our current understanding, these designs seem to be purely decorative, without symbolic associations. As Kroeber continued, "This decoration, which is never realistic, is not

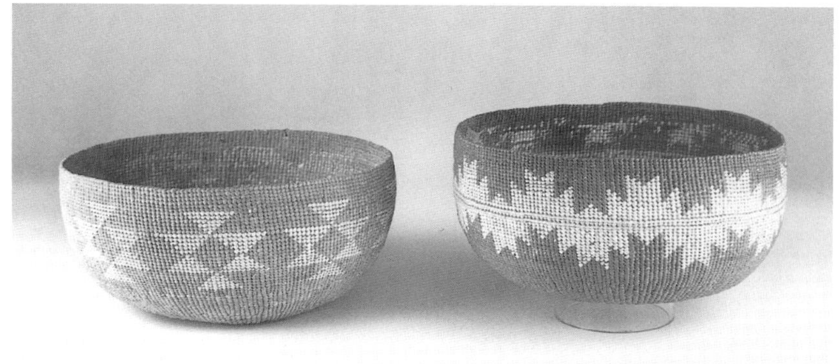

Acorn mush baskets with designs used on purses.

Yurok, 8⅜ in. (21.3 cm.) diameter, 3¾ in. (9.5 cm.) high; collected by Alfred Kroeber in 1901 (1–1472). This is the Spott family design used by Frank Gist on one of his purses.

Hupa (attributed), 7⅞ in. (19.7 cm.) diameter, 3⅝ in. (8.5 cm.) high; collected by Ira Adams before 1971 (1–233740). The same design is on the Yurok purse (1–1427) illustrated in Kelly (plate 113-d).

made with any purpose of signification and usually is nameless; but when a name is applied to it, it is either descriptive, such as 'scratched,' or a name familiar from baskets, such as sitting, sharp-teeth, sturgeon-back, crooked, or mesh-stick" (see also Kelly 1930b:358, O'Neale 1932:74).

Drawing on Kroeber's earlier research (1905), Kelly examined the relation of carving to basket designs (1930b:357). She felt that there was some overlap of designs, especially on the level of motif, but greater divergence characterized the all-over patterns, built-up of individual motifs. Designs common to both forms are the flint, sharp-tooth, sturgeon-back, and crooked patterns. "In general," she concluded, "basketry designs are more varied and complex than those of carving." Obviously the parallel is greater between incised purses and baskets than between the baskets and the spoons and paddles.

We know hardly anything about the ownership of carving designs—if or how they are related to particular individuals/families. Unlike the Northwest Coast, on the Klamath River there was no system of family crests. However, according to Pilling's research, each great house had a distinctive basketry pattern, which marked the house and its property (Pilling 1989:432).

Beyond the issue of "iconography," or the naming of designs, there is the larger question of meaning, what one may call, following the art historian Erwin Panofsky, "iconology." Evidence indicates that for the Yurok, for example, the canoe and house—both large redwood carvings—were considered as living entities. From the Yurok myth recounted by Captain Spott, we learn that the redwood for canoes was once a mythological character, and the named body parts of the canoe reinforce this view. One Yurok told Kroeber that canoes "have sense. If a man leaves his in a bad place and does not take care of it, the canoe knows it and is angry; he will die soon. The canoe causes it. Old men tell young men not to run on the rocks and just leave their boat, nor just leave it anywhere and go off" (Frank 1901:46).[19] According to Yurok author Lucy Thompson, the heart knob was the most important part; without this the canoe was thought to be dead. She likened the placing of the heart to the christening of a vessel (1916:34). The canoe also played a role in Yurok death beliefs, for it transported the soul of a wicked person across the River of Death to purgatory. Significantly, this mortuary vessel lacked the heart. No one would use a canoe without a heart, she wrote, as they believed that it "would be sure to sink or some disaster befall it" (1916:94).

The house, especially the pit, was regarded as the center for family identity (Buckley 1987, Pilling 1989). According to anthropologist Thomas Buckley, "The house was not simply a shelter," but "was considered a sentient being, vibrant with life spirit. Redwood itself was one of the *wogey*, a spirit being, and the redwood planks of a house lived" (1987:10). A good deal of speculation has centered around the symbolism of the house doorway. Nabokov and Easton (1989:290) report that the round hole was regarded as a woodpecker's hole, as a means to force enemies into a helpless posture, or as a symbol of rebirth. This latter interpretation was given by Loren Bommelyn and Sherryl Bommelyn Steinuck (Tolowa): "The doorway of a house in the old days was round, and this represents the womb of the mother. And each night when you go to sleep, you die in a sense. That day that you have lived is in the past. And when you crawl through that door in the morning...you are reborn into that day" (Buckley 1987:10). Whatever the exact meaning, it is clear that Klamath River carving was embued with rich worlds of meaning that we, especially in the non-Native world, can only glimpse.

THE SURVIVAL OF KLAMATH RIVER CARVING (1930–1970)

Alfred Kroeber's fears for the extinction of Native Californian societies proved to be misplaced. Although many aspects of aboriginal cultures clearly declined during much of the twentieth century, the cultures of the Klamath River region continued to live and grow. "For the first third of the twentieth century," noted Bushnell (1968:1111), "the cultural status of the Hupa remained in most essentials the same as in the late 1880s. Many Indian families continued to support themselves by combining hunting, fishing, and gathering with limited farming and stock raising on their land allocations." New foods such as flour, meat, and coffee came to complement rather than supplant the venison, salmon, and acorn soup. Thus, mush paddles and spoons still had a place. Among the new skills that Hupa boys were learning in the local boarding school were carpentry and blacksmithing. Undoubtedly, carving traditions were affected by these new tools and techniques, though exactly how we are not sure. In architecture, there was a gradual shift from the large plank houses to western-style structures of milled lumber (see illustrations in Curtis 1924). Among the Yurok, the menstrual huts were the first to go, followed gradually by the family houses, which lasted into this century. "A few sweathouses lasted a bit longer and today some elders still remember far older men using the sweathouses at *curey* in their childhood, and at *pekwon* until the 1930s" (Buckley 1987:11).

Evidence for the history of Klamath River carving in the period between the publication of Kelly's study in 1930 and the contemporary revival of the 1970s is meager. A revealing glimpse at the continuity of regional traditions can be found in a 1931 letter from Kroeber to his museum colleague Edward Gifford. In discussing a proposed exhibit at the Chicago World's Fair of 1933, Kroeber

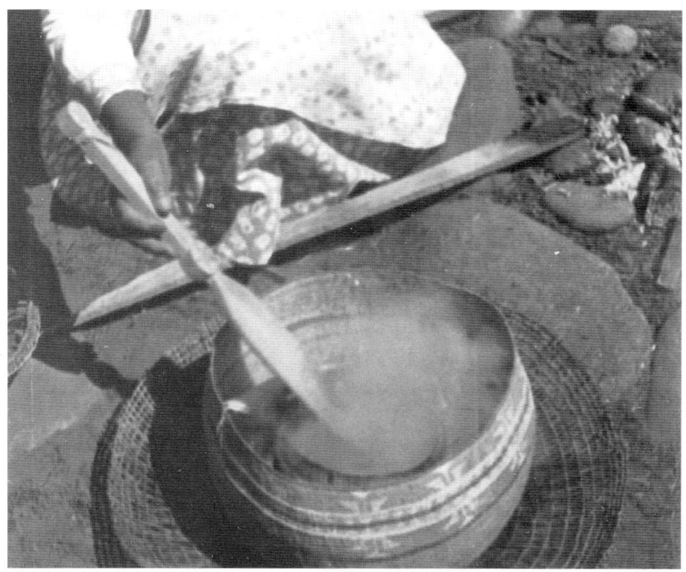

Georgie Henry (Karuk) cooking acorn mush with a mush paddle. *Photograph by Grover Sanderson, Orleans, 1932. (Acc. 2062, print no. 656).*

remarked that "While old-style houses, sweat houses, canoes, etc., are no longer in customary use, there are plenty of Indians on the Klamath that still control the old wood-working techniques, and exceedingly interesting and authentic duplicates could be made" (1931).[20] According to George Blake, elk antler spoons and purses were still being made in the 1940s and 1950s.

For the Hupa, at least, the most dramatic changes came after World War II, with the introduction of electricity and automobiles: "By 1950, after many years of delay, power lines finally reached the reservation, a development that, in combination with their growing prosperity, enabled the Hupa to bring the material side of their culture up-to-date, one might say, almost instantaneously. Television, refrigerators, deep freezers, washers, dryers, and other electrical appliances became standard household equipment for all but the most marginal families" (Bushnell 1968:1113).

By 1970, several observers had noted a definite decline in aboriginal Hupa and Yurok culture. In Hoopa, "The two native plank

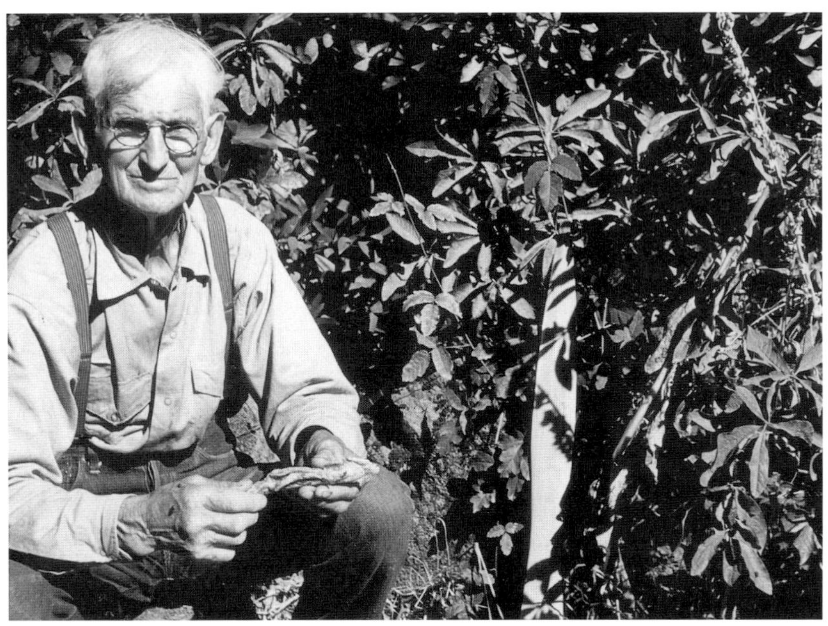

Homer Cooper (Yurok) working on a sinew-backed bow.
Photograph by Samuel Barrett and the American Indian Film Project, Weitchpec, 1959. (Acc. 1983, slide no. 126).

houses preserved on one of the dance grounds were buried by one flood in the mid-1950s and swept away by a second flood during the winter of 1964–65...Although a few canoes and handwoven gill nets were still in use, it had become common practice to catch salmon in a nylon net of modern manufacture, strung across the river channel with the aid of an inflatable life raft or fiberglass boat" (Bushnell 1968:1113). Yurok basketry was a continuous tradition, but there was a reduction in the variety of types made, with a shift from acorn processing forms to the fancy kind, made for sale (Pilling 1978:150). "By 1970," Pilling concluded, "none of the traditional major ceremonies was being performed on Yurok territory, nor had any been held at a traditional Yurok site since 1939." Furthermore, "In 1972, very few traditional Yurok regalia technologists survived" (1978:148).

Just when things seemed bleakest, however, there was a strong "renaissance" of Klamath River culture in the mid-1960s. Acorn soup was still made occasionally, especially for dances. The Hupa continued to dance, and a new sweathouse was erected in 1965 prior to the annual Brush Dance as a replacement for the one lost in the flood. Girls learned basket weaving in high school, and many cultural projects led to the establishment of the Hoopa Tribal Museum in 1974 (Bushnell 1968:1114–15). In the early 1970s, Yurok dancing underwent a revival (Pilling 1978:148).

Carving was included in this renaissance. According to Arnold Pilling (1978:150), "As late as 1970, several elderly Yurok woodworkers survived. The technological knowledge for the construction of a traditional house, dugout, stool, bow, and some fishing items was still present and such items were occasionally made. Although most of these woodworkers were born before 1910, a few men younger than 30 commanded the skills for house construction, mush-paddle carving, and possibly those for dugout construction." Unfortunately, Pilling does not name these individuals, but chief among the senior generation were probably Homer Cooper (c. 1880–c. 1975), Dewey George (1899–1987), and Haynes Moore (1900–early 1970s).

In October and November of 1960, Samuel Barrett filmed several of these carvers at work: Haynes Moore carving a dugout canoe and Homer Cooper making an elk antler spoon and wedge and a sinew-backed bow and arrow set (Barrett 1961b). When Barrett arrived at Moore's work-site near Pekwan, he found one finished canoe and another three in various stages of construction, certainly a sign of an active carving tradition, at least for canoes. In fact, Moore had spent much of his life, beginning around 1940, making canoes. After moving to Hoopa in 1953, he taught boat building, with modern as well as traditional tools, at the local high school (see Ortiz 1990:14). Another documented canoe from this period was the one carved in 1968 by Dewey George and Jimmy James (b. 1914). (Carved on commission for Paul's Cannery in Klamath, it is now on exhibit at the Redwood National Park information center in Orick.) Dewey George continued to teach canoe-making into the 1970s (Cunningham 1989:59, Parkman 1987:8).

It is hard to know how much experience Homer Cooper had with elk antler spoon-making; possibly, he had never made one before.[21] What is clear is Barrett's archaistic interests. Although Cooper

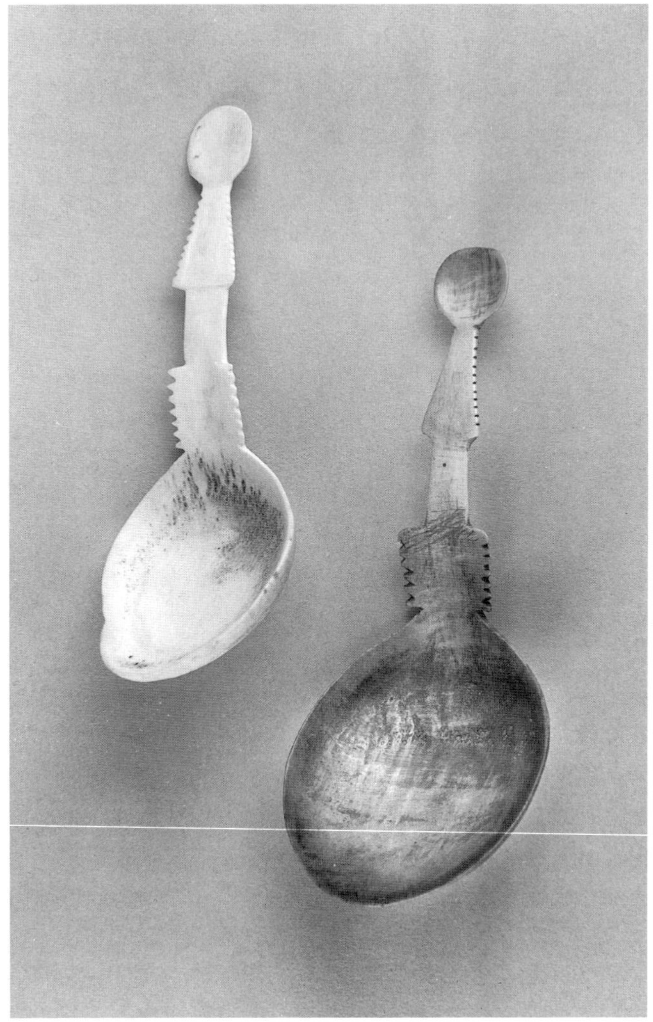

Acorn mush spoons, elk antler.

Yurok, made by Homer Cooper in November of 1960, 4⅜ in. (11.2 cm.) long, 2⅛ in. (5.3 cm.) wide at the bowl, collected by Samuel A. Barrett for the American Indian Film Project (1–198154).

Hupa original, which Barrett asked Cooper to copy, 4¾ in. (12.1 cm.) long, 2¾ in. (7.0 cm.) wide at the bowl; collected by Philip M. Jones in 1901 (1–795). Note the darker color (from tannic acid in acorn mush) and larger bowl (from bigger elk) of the older spoon.

preferred to use store-bought glue for his bows, the Berkeley anthropologist insisted that he reconstruct the old ways (1961a:157–58). Similarly, he supplied him with the "elk antler wedges, maul, and adze to demonstrate the old time system of working wood" (1960–62:19). Noting that Homer Cooper "has an old antler upon which he is going to experiment," Barrett "left him one of our greener and fresher antlers with which to do the final work for us" (1960–62:50). In the final footage, preserved in Hearst Museum archives, one sees Cooper forming the spoon solely by cutting with obsidian and rubbing against a hard stone. Viewing this footage recently, George Blake commented sardonically that carvers had been using iron-tipped tools for over a century, and it seemed wrong that Cooper should have to work so hard, solely to please the preconceived notions of the anthropologist.

According to Blake, Homer Cooper began a new career in the 1960s. He had been a rancher in the Eureka area, but after retirement returned to making old-style objects: "Cooper, an old Indian guy, went back in his sixties and began to really delve into the culture, do all of what he remembered, and then when he didn't remember he'd begin to make things in other ways." He was known for his tanning, women's dresses, and sinew-backed bows, but did little carving as his manual dexterity had declined with the years. Blake remembered that "his house was like a museum." Homer Cooper, Dewey George, and Haynes Moore were three leading Klamath River carvers who maintained the art form into the late twentieth century. That they made creative adaptations as times changed did not make their work any less authentic. It was from this base that the current revival sprang.

THE ART TODAY

The work of people like George, Cooper, and Moore paved the way for the current revival in Klamath River carving, associated most notably with the work of George Blake (Hupa/Yurok) and Frank Gist (Yurok). Although there are many others who have carved or still do some carving, few specialize in it to the extent that these men do. As in former times, almost all carvers are male.

The senior carver today is George Blake (Hupa/Yurok). Born in

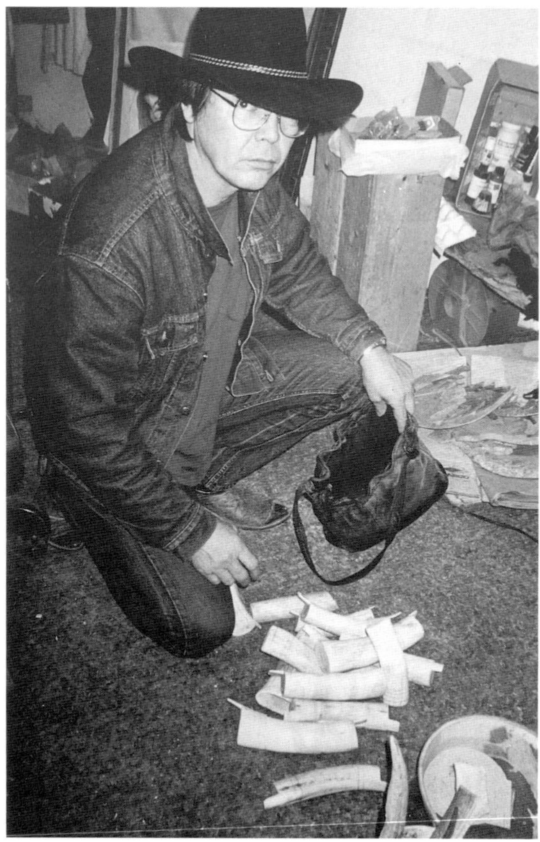

George Blake in his studio, Hoopa, California.
Photograph by Ira Jacknis, January, 1995.

1944 on the Hoopa Indian Reservation, he still resides there today. Although he has a Yurok father and Hupa mother, he tends to affiliate himself more with his Hupa heritage. After high school, Blake served in Europe with the U.S. Army (1963–66). Before college (College of the Redwoods, 1973–75, University of California at Davis, B.A. in Fine Arts and Native American Art, 1978), he spent two years as a traveling missionary for the Indian Shaker faith. From 1980 to 1984 he served as director of the Hoopa Tribal Museum, and since then has made his living as a full-time artist. Widely exhibited across the country and a frequent demonstrator of his art, he was a 1991 recipient of a National Heritage Fellowship from the Folk Arts

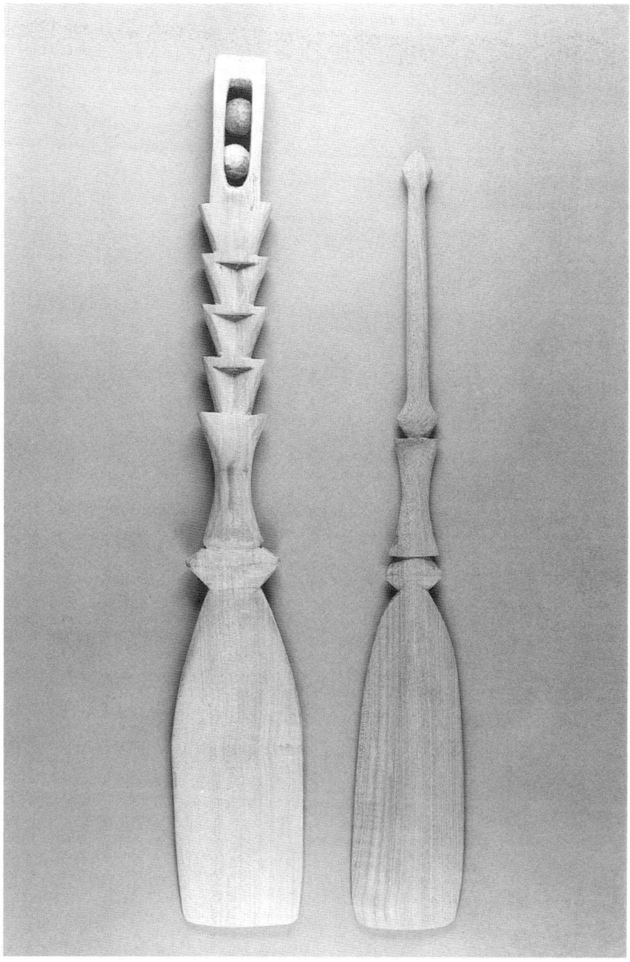

Acorn mush paddles by George Blake. Maple wood.

Handle with carved wooden balls inside, 1995; 27 in. (68.5 cm.) long, 4⅜ in. (10.5 cm.) wide at the paddle (1–259291). This is an especially elaborate version. Blake said that he had a great uncle who made paddle handles like this. This was an innovation in Klamath River carving, probably stimulated by contact with whites; but according to Blake, such carving has been done on the Klamath River for at least a century now, since the introduction of metal-tipped tools. Blake has made several more like this. He considers the triangle cut-outs along the handle, giving a "shadow effect," to be his own, personal, design.

1994; 24⅜ in. (62 cm.) long,
3½ in (8.8 cm.) wide at the paddle (1–259286).

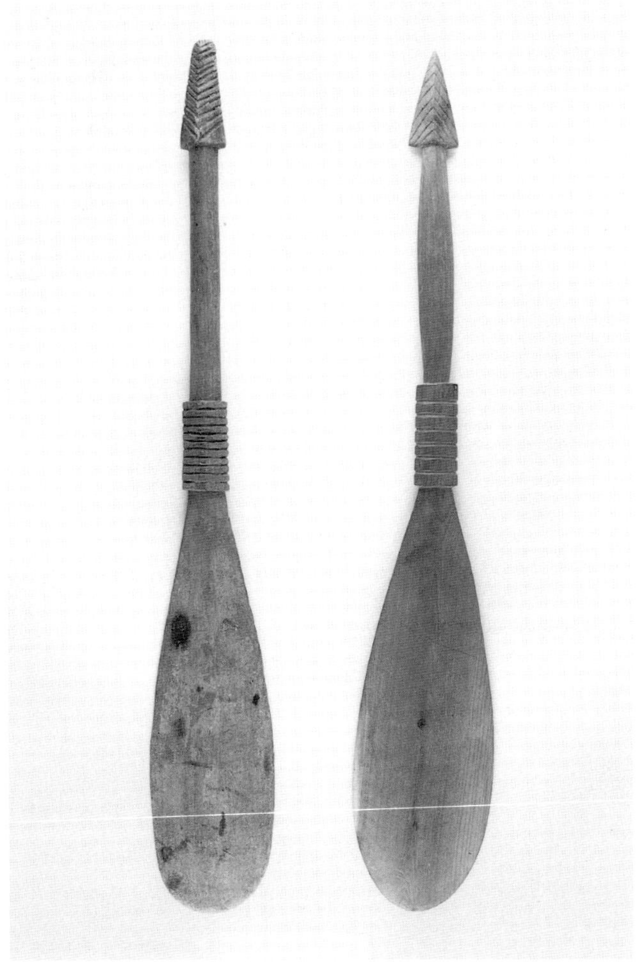

Hupa acorn mush paddle; 17¼ in. (43.7 cm.) long; collected by Philip M. Jones in 1901 (1–922). Blake first saw this old Hupa paddle on a visit to the Hearst Museum during his directorship of the Hoopa Tribal Museum; he liked it so much that he made two copies of it.

Acorn mush paddle by George Blake, 1982; 17¼ in. (43.7 cm.) long (1–259272).

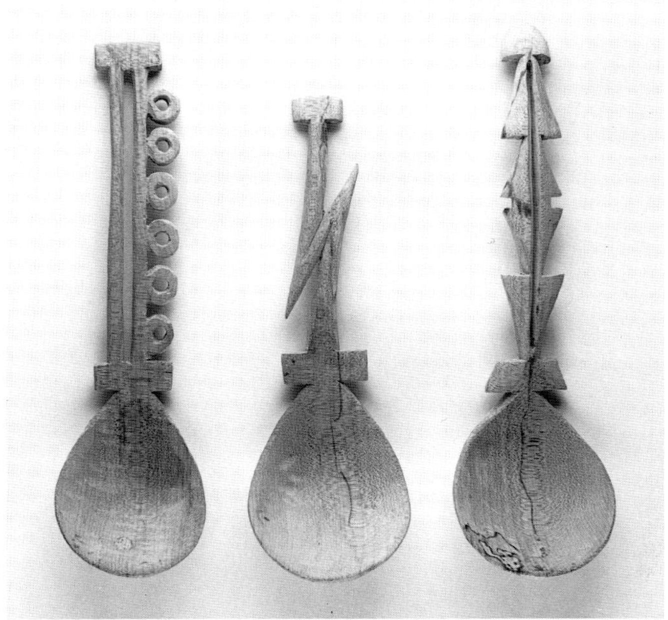

Acorn mush spoons by George Blake, 1995. Maple wood.
Slot and circle design, 7⅝ in. (19.3 cm.) long (1–259288).
Zigzag design, 6⅞ in. (17.6 cm.) long (1–259290).
Slot and triangle design, 8 in. (20.3 cm.) long (1–259289).
Blake usually carves wooden spoons in large quantities at a time.

program of the National Endowment for the Arts. He works both in contemporary styles of ceramics, jewelry, sculpture, and painting, and in traditional forms and media such as redwood canoes, sinew-backed bow and arrow sets, elk antler purses and spoons, and ceremonial featherwork.

Although George Blake had always been good with his hands, he began to carve seriously in the 1960s, while still in high school and living with his aunt, Lila Colegrove. "That's how I got started making acorn spoons, and that's how I got started in the art work. When she started making baskets, and they needed acorn spoons, I said, 'I've got to be able to make a spoon on a band saw.'" Blake made a set of wooden spoons for the feast and, as he joked, "Since then I've had a band saw all my life, and I've made acorn spoons ever since then."

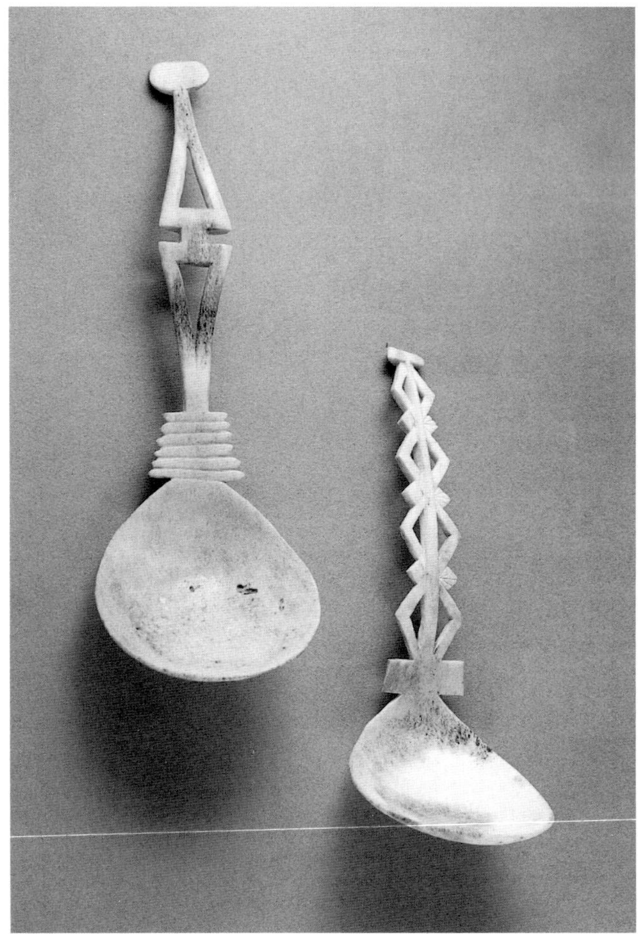

Acorn mush spoons by George Blake. Elk antler.

1991, 8⅜ in. (21.2 cm.) long. Private collection. Blake carved this for the *A Dialogue with Tradition* exhibition at The Brooklyn Museum. This is one of Blake's favorite spoon designs.

1994, 6¾ in. (17.2 cm.) long, (1–295275). Blake considers this one of his best spoons.

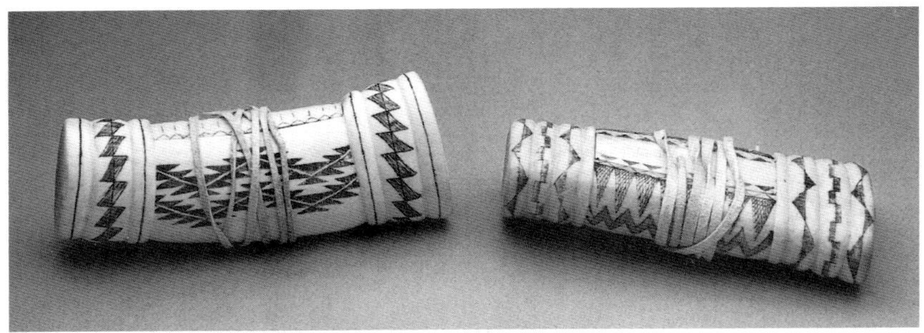

Purses by George Blake, 1995. Elk antler, black pigment, hide. Vertical, with basket design, 5¾ in. (14.6 cm.) long (1–259270). Horizontal, 5½ in. (14.0 cm.) long (1–259269). Purses commonly come in these two formats, depending on how the antler naturally sits and where the opening is placed on the purse.

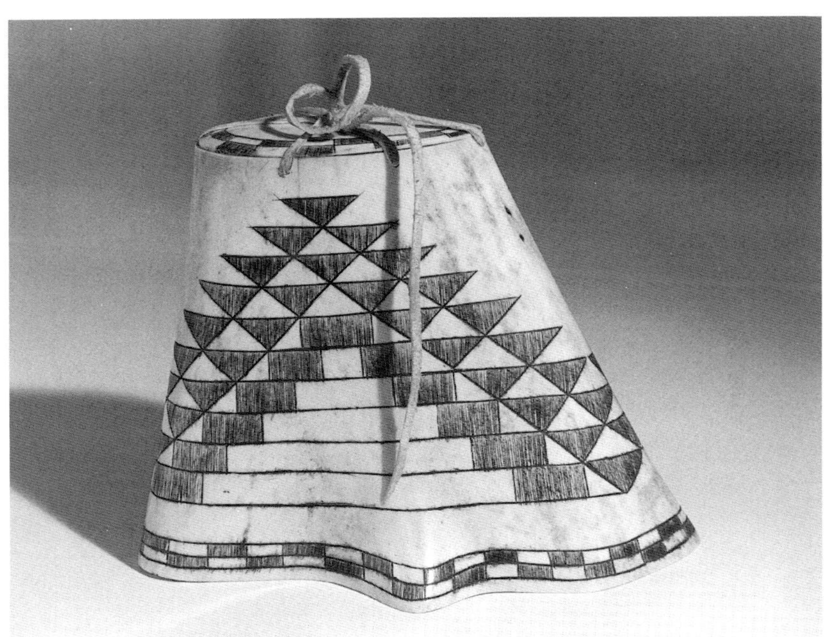

Upright-style purse by George Blake, 1991. Elk antler, black pigment, hide, 5 in. (12.7 cm.) high, 6¾ in. (17.2 cm.) wide. Artist's collection. Made for display at the exhibition *A Dialogue with Tradition* at The Brooklyn Museum. Although not directly inspired by older models, this purse is a more elaborate version of similar examples in the Hearst Museum.

One of Blake's youthful desires was to make a sinew-backed bow (see Ortiz 1995:30–33). Although the last Hupa bow-maker (James Hostler) lived nearby, by the time Blake was ready he had died, so Blake's grandfather suggested he talk to Homer Cooper. Inspired by the work and his contact with Dewey George and Homer Cooper, Blake learned traditional crafts largely on his own. As Blake recalled Cooper's teaching methods, "Well, he didn't teach me. He told me things, and how things were made. And he was careful, he almost was checking my interest. If I was interested enough to try it on my own, and if I failed, he'd show me."[22] Inspired by one of Cooper's elk antler purses, Blake began to make them around 1968. After years carving wooden spoons, in the mid-1980s Blake tried his hand at elk antler spoons. When he first starting making them, elk antler spoons had probably not been made since Homer Cooper's work in the early 1960s. Although these traditional forms are still vitally important to him, today George Blake concentrates on ceramics, jewelry and, recently, sculpture. Blake has been selling his work as long as he has been making it, but has only been supporting himself as a full-time artist since leaving the Hoopa Museum in 1984.

A decade younger than Blake, Frank G. Gist, Jr. (Yurok) was born in Willits, California, in 1954. At the age of four, he moved to Crescent City, north of the Klamath River, to live with his great-aunt Minnie Spott Macomber, who taught him about his cultural heritage. Also living with them for a time was Minnie's sister, Little Alice, and their mother, Alice Spott (c. 1880–1963). Alice Spott was one of Kroeber's principal Yurok consultants, and it must have been a special experience to be brought up by this woman who embodied so much of aristocratic Yurok culture. Frank Gist studied at Oakland's Merritt College in 1972–73. In 1973, he left California upon joining the Army (82nd Airborne Division, 1975–79). His Army experience as a dental hygienist, 1979–82, came in handy when he turned to carving. Upon leaving the service in 1982, Frank Gist settled in Sacramento. Between 1984 and 1989, he worked for the Urban Indian Health project. Since then he has been employed by the County of Sacramento as an Eligibility Worker for AFDC (Aid for Families with Dependent Children), where he handles the cases of American Indian families.

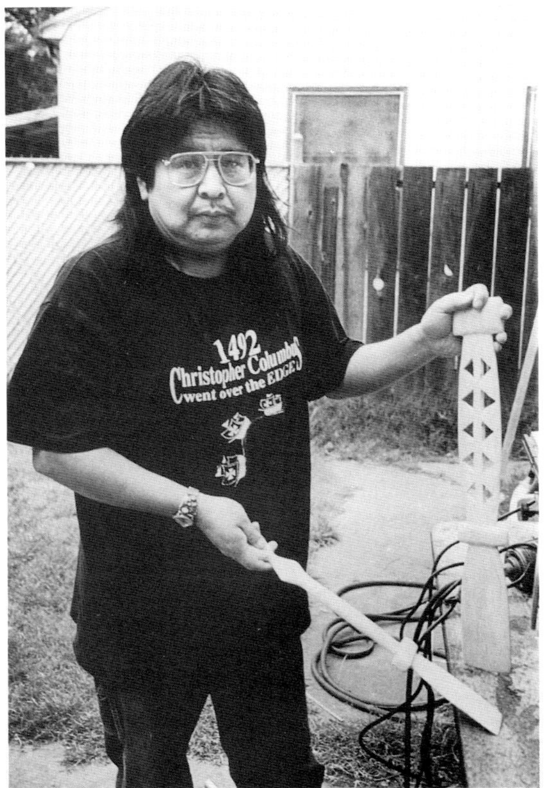

Frank Gist in his work area at the back
of his house, Sacramento, California.
Photograph by Ira Jacknis, March, 1995.

Self-taught as a carver, Gist works at his craft in the evenings and weekends. He has been making traditional Yurok objects since about 1982. Among his principal products are spoons and purses of elk antler, wooden mush paddles and spoons, pipes, and drums. Gist's first piece was probably the purse he made for his aunt: "I got interested [about twelve years ago]. My aunt...gave me an elk horn, and she said, 'I want a purse out of it.' I said I'd try. It took me a whole year to make that first purse, because nobody ever taught me how... I just picked it up through trial and error" (Ortiz 1994:18). Gist studied purses in museums and books. "Just recently," he continued, "after about ten years, I gave my aunt her purse. And she about cried. I said, 'I didn't want to give you that first one because it didn't look

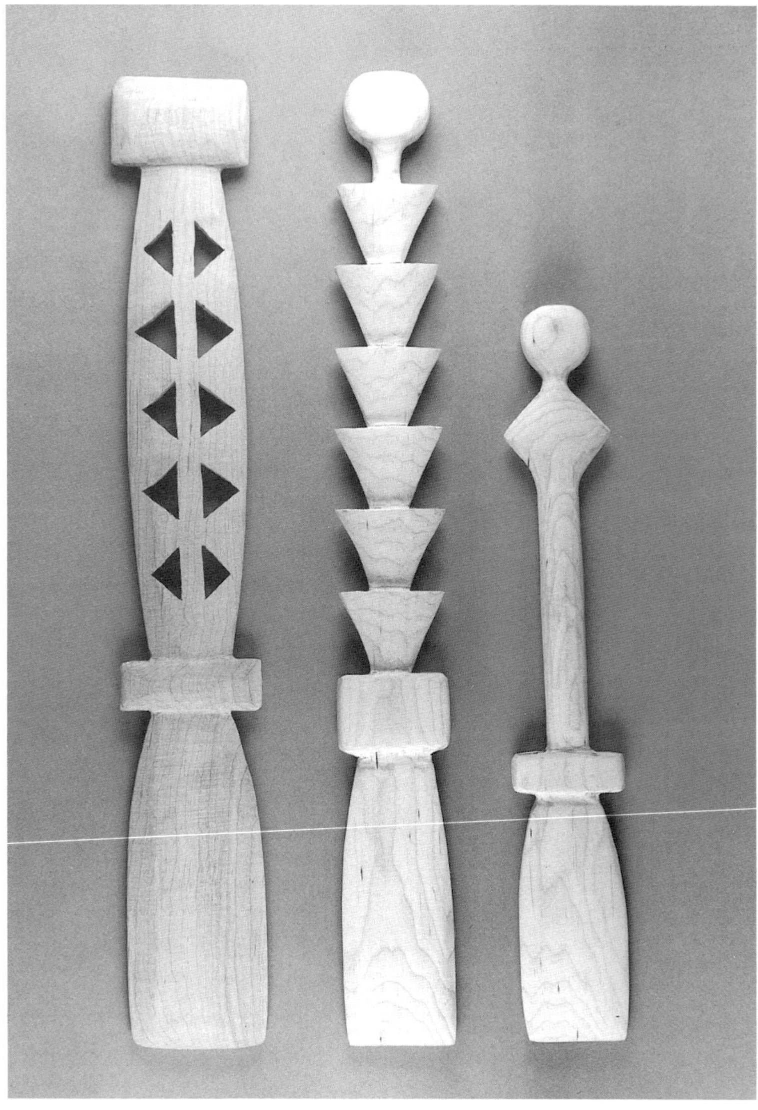

Acorn mush paddles by Frank Gist, 1995. Maple wood.

Handle with diamond cut-outs is Gist's version of Yurok paddle (1–2035) illustrated in Kelly, plate 112d; 24 in. (61 cm.) long, 3½ in. (8.8 cm.) wide at paddle (1–259279).

Handle with stacked triangles is called a sturgeon-back design; 23⅞ in. (60.5 cm.) long, 2¾ in. (6.9 cm.) wide at paddle (1–259280).

Right handle has no known design name; 18 in. (45.5 cm.) long, 2⅝ in. (6.7 cm.) wide at paddle (1–259281).

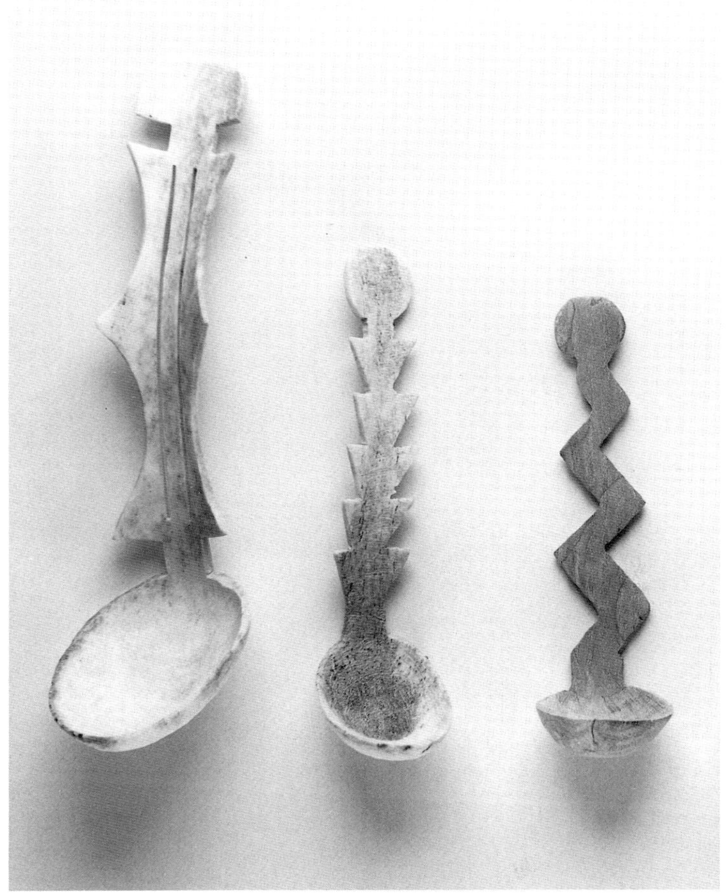

Acorn mush spoons, by Frank Gist, 1995.

Large elk antler spoon is Gist's version of a Klamath River spoon design (1–1238, illustrated in Kelly, plate 103b) that was a favorite of the artist's great-aunt Minnie Spott Macomber; 6¾ in. (17.2 cm.) long (1–259284).

Smaller elk antler spoon, with sturgeon-back design, 4½ in. (11.4 cm.) long. Artist's collection.

Zigzag design, maple wood, 5 in. (12.7 cm.) long (1–259267).

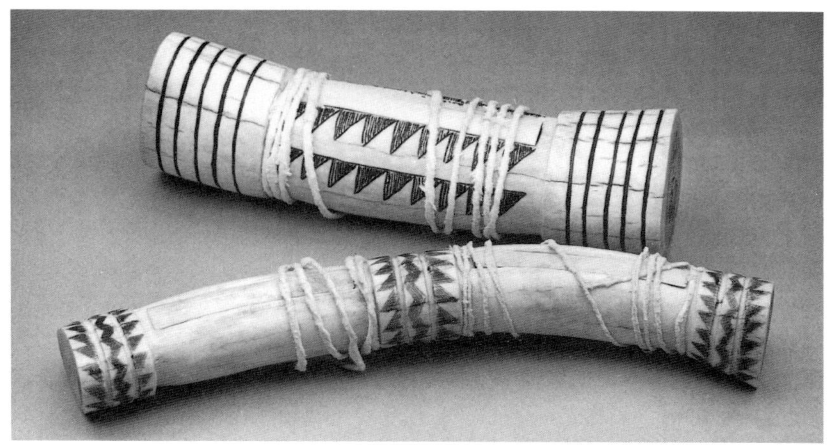

Purses by Frank Gist, 1995. Elk antler, black pigment, hide. Artist's collection.

Larger purse, 7½ in. (19.0 cm.) long.

Double-slotted, 8¾ in. (22.2 cm.) long. Gist was inspired to make the double-slotted purse, a very unusual form, from a Klamath River example (1–1251) in Kelly's book (plate 117d). Note, however, how different is his design.

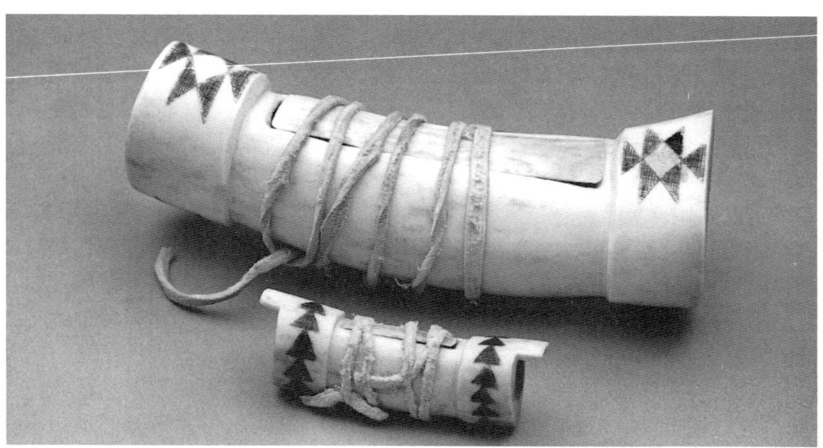

Purses by Frank Gist, 1994. Elk antler, black pigment, hide.

Spott family design, 6¼ in. (15.6 cm.) long (1–259266).

Miniature, 2⅞ in. (7.2 cm.) long. Private collection. Miniatures, which are smaller and cheaper, have become especially popular in the contemporary market.

right. I wanted to give you one that I felt really good about. It's just the way it should be...' "

Both Blake and Gist are active teachers. Frank Gist teaches at the State Indian Museum and for the Indian Education Program, both in Sacramento. George Blake has taught on the Hoopa Reservation and at Humboldt State University in Arcata. One of Blake's protégés, Tim Bussell (Hupa, b. 1951) is a full-time auto mechanic who has been making purses for about ten years, off and on. Bussell has made boats, feathered regalia, and silver jewelry, but he found his forte when he began helping Blake fit tight lids onto purses. Recently he has started putting colored pigment, especially red, into the incised lines of his purses. As he explained, "The color just needed to be there; it grabs you, pulls you to it." An even greater use of color can be found in a purse by Blake's nephew, Caw-tep Sylvia (Hupa/Yurok, b. 1975). Red, yellow, blue, and green highlight the freely rendered, abstract designs, some derived from basketry. Although he has studied with Blake, young Sylvia derives some of his innovative style from the work of his father, Chuffy Sylvia.

Like many forms of Native American art, there has been a shift in function of some kinds of Klamath River carving from use in traditional Native life to a fine arts market for non-Natives. As in basketry, there has been a reduction in the scope of forms produced, yet it is surprising how many traditional object types are still being made in some fashion. The principal forms produced today are the canoe, mush paddle, spoon of antler and wood, purse, and pipe. Today, no one lives in the old plank houses, although several are still used ceremonially, and a traditional village has recently been constructed as a public display at Sumeg Yurok Village, Patrick's Point State Park (Parkman 1987, 1991). Canoes are most often made for display, but they are used occasionally for travel, and they still play a role in the Boat Dance. Mush paddles and spoons are still used for the feasts associated with the annual world renewal dances, but given the rarity and difficulty of using elk antler, the spoons are usually made of wood. Although the system of dentalium money has largely collapsed, purses are still used occasionally to hold dentalia in ceremonial transactions. They have gained a secondary function as containers for jewelry and

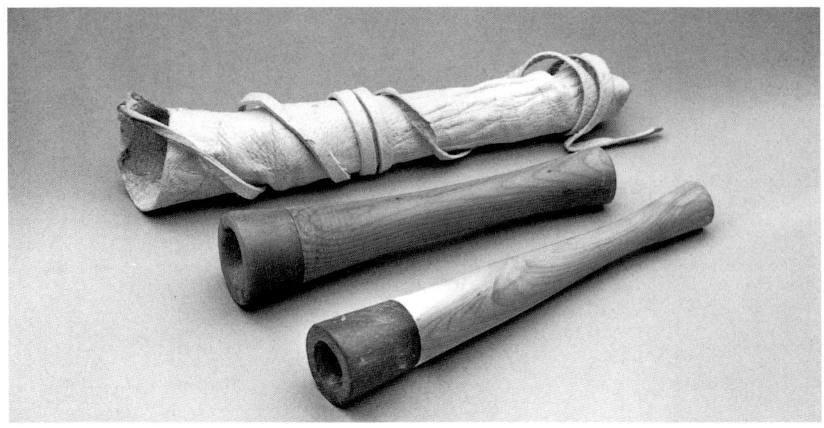

Pipe by George Blake, 1995. Manzanita wood stem and blue-green soapstone bowl, with white deerhide case, 5⅜ (13.2 cm.) long, 1⅛ in. (2.8 cm.) diameter at the bowl (1–259292).

Pipe by Frank Gist, 1995. Yew stem and black soapstone bowl, 6⅛ in. (15.5 cm.) long, ⅞ in. (2.4 cm.) diameter at the bowl (1–259285).

Unlike the pipes of the nineteenth century, these were turned on the lathe.

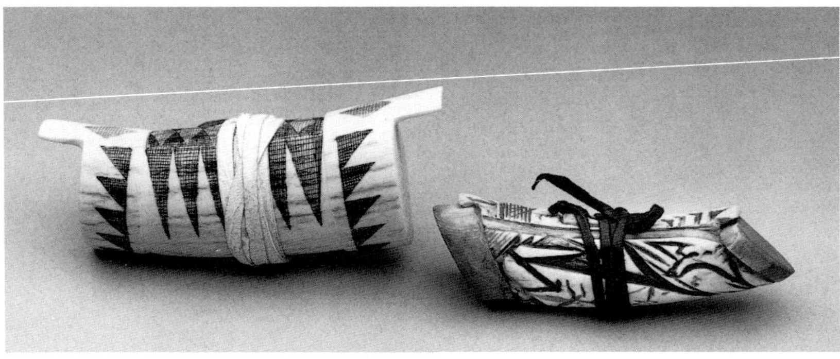

Purse by Tim Bussell, Sr. (Hupa), 1995; elk antler, red and black pigment, hide; 5 in. (12.7 cm.) long (1–259297).

Purse by Caw-tep Sylvia (Hupa/Yurok), George Blake's nephew, 1995, elk antler, yew wood, pigments (red, yellow, green, blue), 3¾ in. (9.5 cm.) long. Collection of Annabelle Blake.

These pieces are by two of Blake's students.

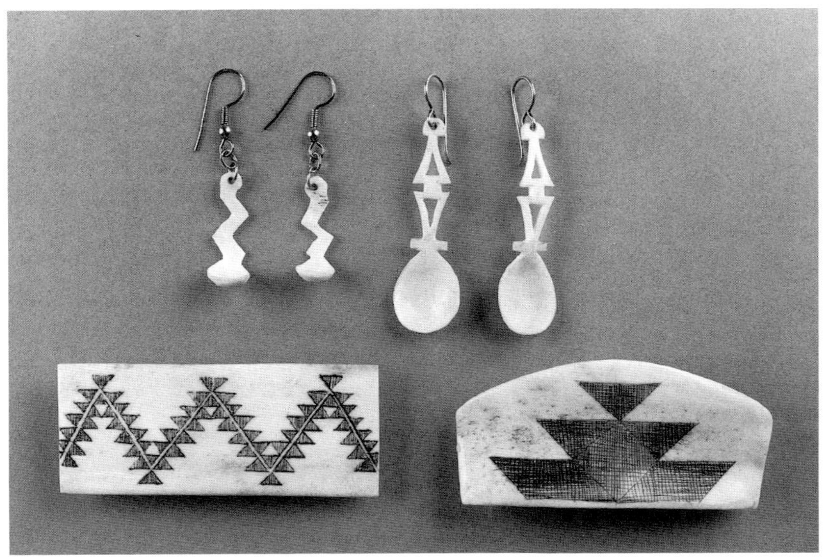

Jewelry. Elk antler with metal fasteners.

Spoon earrings by Frank Gist, 1994, ⅞ in. (2.2 cm.) long, antler only (1–259089).

Spoon earrings by George Blake, 1994, 1⅞ in. (4.8 cm.) long (1–259276).

Pin by George Blake, 1994, with flying geese design, 2⅞ in. (7.3 cm.) long, 1⅛ in. (2.8 cm.) wide (1–259277).

Hair clip by Tim Bussell, 1994, 3⅞ in. (9.8 cm.) long, 1¼ in. (3.2 cm.) wide (1–259268).

The elk antler material and traditional spoon handle and basketry designs have been adapted for contemporary jewelry.

medicines. Pipes are sometimes used, especially for doctoring. Most of these forms, however, are made for sale.

As with California basketry, Klamath River carvers today encounter problems in obtaining suitable materials. The elk is a rare species, not common in the region except in a few areas of park land. Even when present, because of hunting pressure through much of its range, they are not allowed to fully mature before they are killed (Petersen 1988:52). Thus most of the antler available today is markedly smaller than a century ago. Because the size of a spoon's

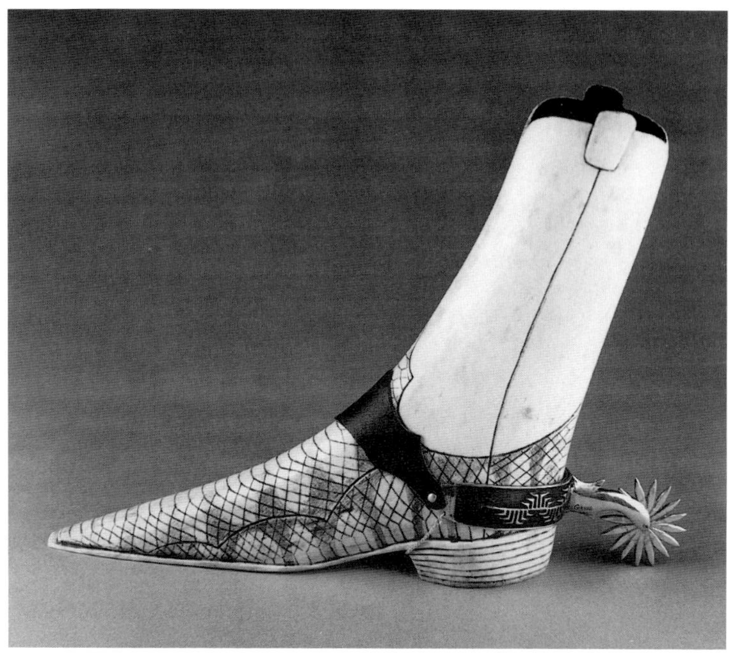

Sculpture: "Dude Boot," by George Blake, 1995. Elk antler, silver, and black leather, with interior velvet flocking, 8½ in. (21.6 cm.) high, 11⅜ in. (28.8 cm.) long, including spur. Artist's collection. This innovative piece, which depicts the cowboy boots that Blake loves to wear, was inspired by the natural shape of the elk antler.

bowl is limited by the diameter of the antler at the skull, smaller antlers will necessitate smaller spoons. Because of extensive logging, there is a similar problem with obtaining proper sizes and kinds of old-growth redwood critical for canoe-carving. This has led George Blake to employ logs from the smaller second-growth, and Blake thinks, if necessary, "future generations down the road...might have to make a dugout canoe with 4 x 4s laminated....'Cause they're using up all the redwood" (Ortiz 1990:16).

Generally, there has been a diminution of designs over the twentieth century. As in other areas of Native North America (Zuni pottery, for example; Batkin 1987:82), collecting has removed visual sources from Native villages. An artist growing up cannot see a wide range of designs but has to come to museums or rely on publications (for the

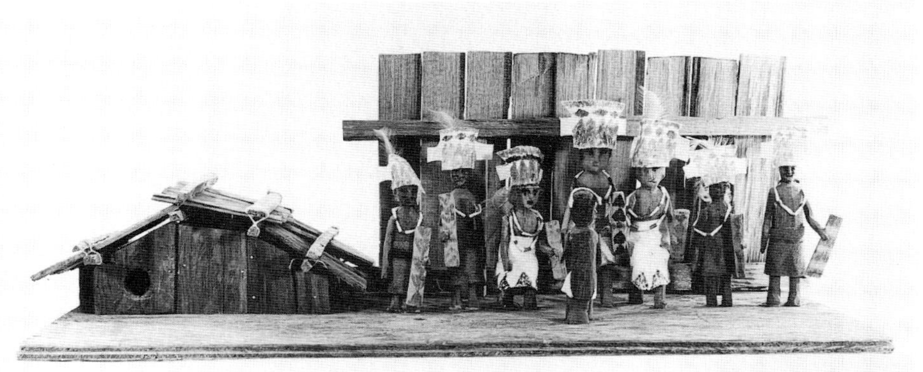

Model of a Jump Dance, by Dewey George (Yurok), 1969. Redwood, buckskin, feathers, glass beads, dentalia shells, clam shells, ink, paint, nails, cotton string, glue, and plywood, 26¼ in. (66.6 cm.) long at the plywood base, 14¼ in. (36.2 cm.) wide at the plywood base, 9¼ in. (23.5 cm.) high. George made many such models in the 1960s; this one shows a Yurok family house, dance pit, and dancers. End of the Trail Museum, Trees of Mystery, Klamath, California. Photograph by Bruce Van Meter.

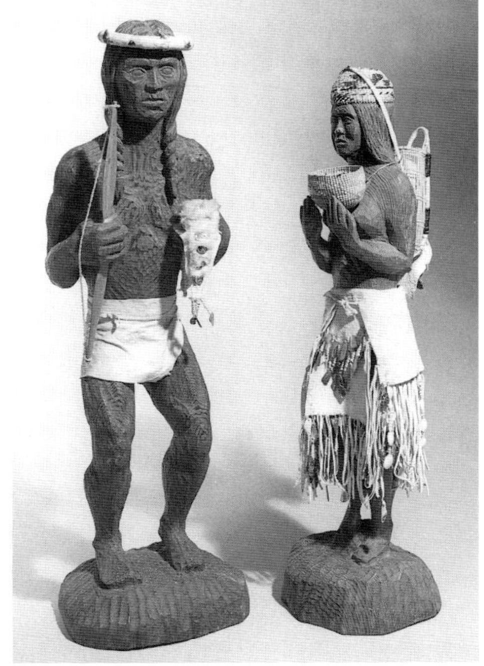

Sculpture: "Just a Fond Memory," male and female dancers, by George Blake, c. 1972. Miniature mush basket by Amy Peters (Yurok), miniature basketry cap by Ollie James (Yurok), miniature baby basket by Ina Faustino (Yurok). Redwood, basketry (spruce roots, willow roots, hazel and willow shoots, bear grass, maidenhair fern), deerskin, deer sinew, mink fur (?), woodpecker feathers, cedar wood, abalone shells, clam shells, glass seed beads, waxed nylon. Male figure: 20¼ in. (51.5) high; female figure: 18¼ in. (46.3 cm.). Artist's collection. Inspired by the figures of Dewey George, Blake made these before going to college.

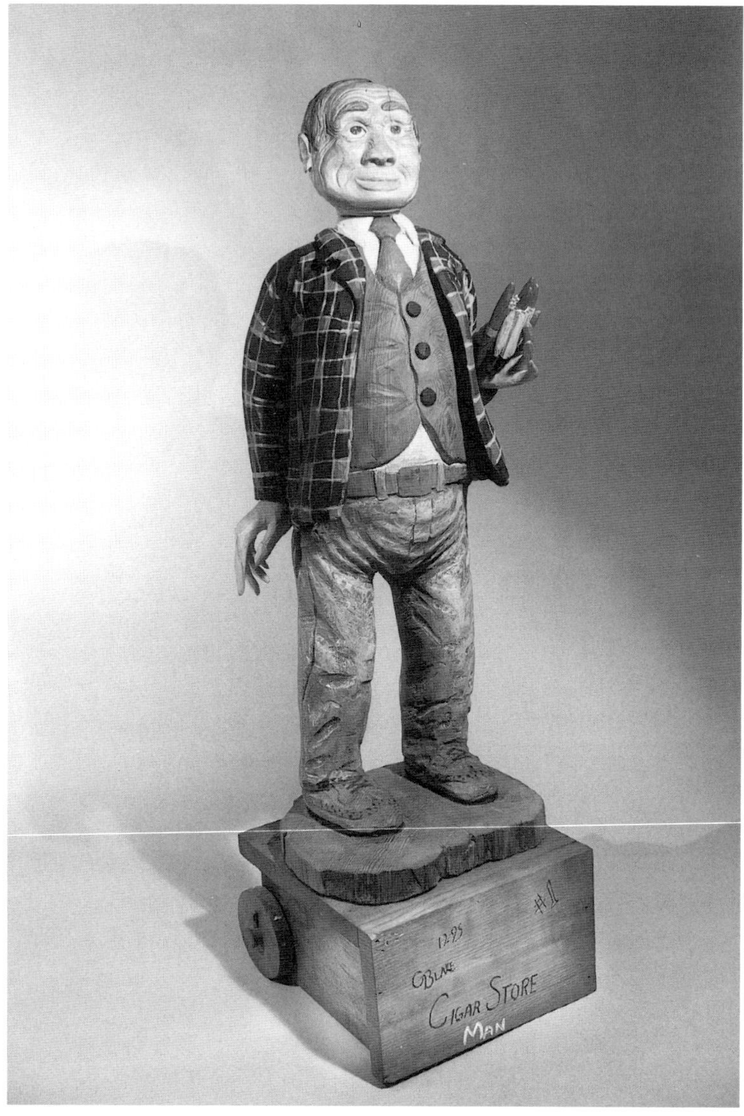

Sculpture: "Cigar Store White Man, no. 1," by George Blake, 1995. Redwood, Port Orford cedar, paint, 41¾ in. (106.0 cm.) high, including base. Artist's collection. Blake enjoys poking fun at racial and cultural stereotypes. He modeled the face after popular singer Mel Tormé and the hands after a Balinese carving. His brother-in-law, who had fashion experience, helped with the plaid jacket. The first in a projected series, this was meant to be a maquette version for a full-size figure.

Northwest Coast, see Blackman and Hall 1982). Accordingly, Isabel Kelly's study—usually in photocopied form—has had a great impact. It has been the major source for Gist's spoon designs, and Blake, too, commonly uses spoon designs from the Hearst collection that were illustrated in Kelly. The much greater variety in purse designs may be due to the relative freedom allowed by the decorated surface. One of the most important changes has been the common use of women's basketry designs on purses, which once were decorated with a fairly separate stock of geometric motifs. George Blake uses basketry designs on much of his work, including ceramics and silver jewelry, because he regards these as distinctive parts of his culture and wants to keep the designs alive. On his purses, Frank Gist also uses family basketry designs.

Another direction of Klamath River carving in recent years has been the development of sculpture, as fine art in the Western sense. In Native California, painters and graphic artists such as Harry Fonseca, Frank LaPena, and Jean LaMarr have achieved greater notoriety than sculptors (LaPena and Driesbach 1985). Despite Powers' observation of "crude" figures in the nineteenth century, there had been no regional tradition of figurative sculpture. In the mid-1960s, Dewey George made several sets of small wooden figures depicting ceremonial scenes: a model house and Jump Dance, and the Boat Dance from the White Deerskin Dance.[23] George, one of the last priests of a great house, may have turned to ceremonial scenes because of his great expertise at regalia-making (Pilling 1989:429, 431–32). Inspired by these figures, George Blake began his work in figurative sculpture, a genre that he has continued to the present. In the early 1970s, before enrolling in college, Blake created a pair of costumed redwood figures, representing a male and female dancer. Drawing on his fine art training, George Blake has continued to create sculpture of clay, wood, and bronze. His sculptural work is often satiric, linking him with his colleague and Davis teacher David Gilhooly, known for his ceramic sculpture, and the Bay Area Funk movement of the 1960s and 1970s.

Although both are primarily graphic artists, other sculptors from the region are Rick E. Bartow (Yurok) and Brian D. Tripp (Karuk). Although Bartow's grandfather was Yurok, he has lived most of his

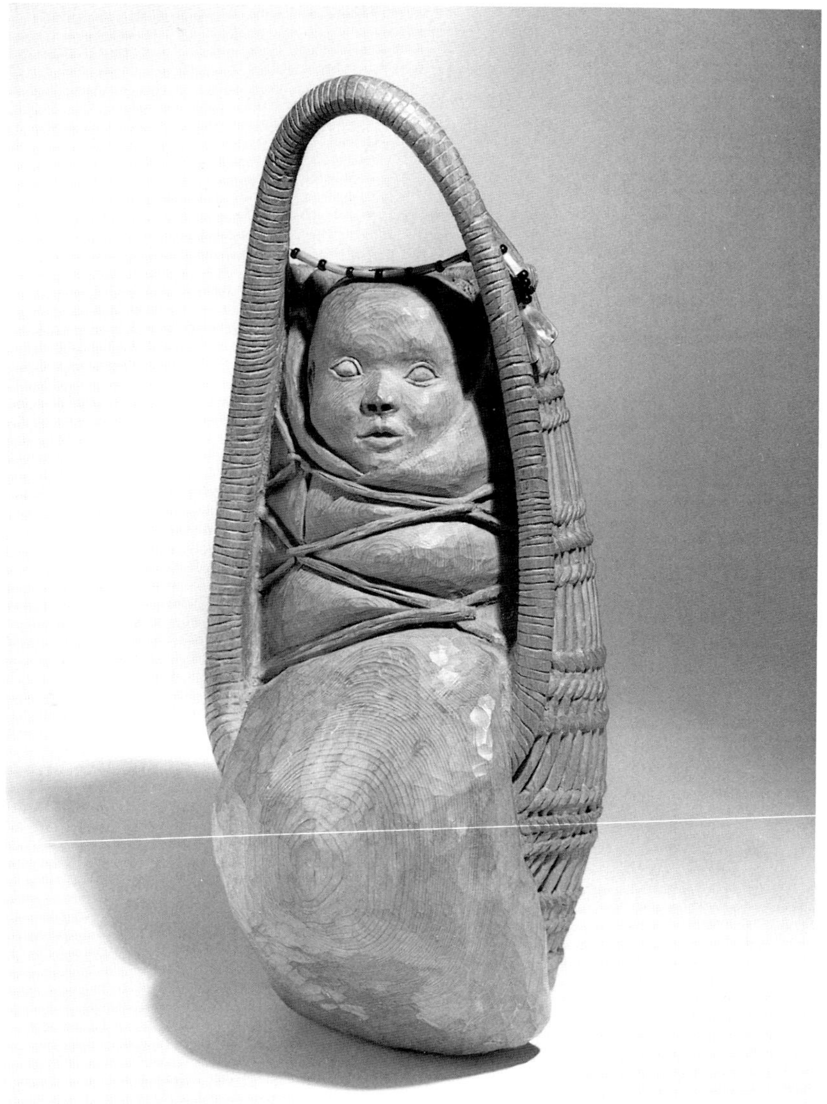

Sculpture: "Baby in a Basket," by George Blake, 1974–87. Port Orford cedar, shell and glass beads, 16⅝ in. (42.2 cm.) high. Artist's collection. Blake found that it was taking him so much time to carve out the basketry cradle at the back that he put it aside. Years later, needing a piece for an exhibition, he picked it up again and completed it. He says that children love to touch it; in fact, the beaded cord along the top was originally carved out of wood, but it was broken by his daughter.

life in the Oregon communities of Ocean Beach and Newport, where he was born in 1946. After earning a B.A. from Western Oregon State College in Monmouth in 1969, Bartow was sent to Vietnam. Later he learned to use Northwest Coast style carving tools (from British Columbia), and about 1982 began to carve masks from cedar, as well as other more abstract sculptures (Wasserman 1986). Born in Eureka in 1945, Tripp studied and taught art at Humboldt State University (LaPena and Driesbach 1985:66–67; Johnson, Roth, and Tani 1992). Since about 1985, he has been working in more sculptural forms, much of which incorporates painting and found objects. In all his work, Tripp combines a strong abstract sense with motifs and themes taken from Karuk ceremonialism and basketry.

It has now been over sixty years since Isabel Kelly prepared her review of the carver's art of the Klamath River Indians. Since that time the carving traditions of the region have experienced an exciting regeneration. With the aid of new tools and patient study, carvers today are producing works that equal and even surpass the high creative achievements of the last century. It is past time, then, to review the craft, history, and cultural context of this art, but this essay is only the first, not the last, word. It is our hope that the current exhibition and publication can help fulfill George Blake's desire to "give the Indian community a chance to look at the wealth of things that were picked up from the area where we're from, and a chance to actually just look and research by looking at it. There's a real interest in carving right now, and a document of these things back into the community could only help. I want to bring that excitement back to the people."

NOTES

1. Information in this essay attributed to the two Native curators was gathered primarily in formal interviews with George Blake (December 26, 1990; January 3–4, 21, 1995; February 9–11, 1995), and Frank Gist (October 1, 26, 1994; March 10–11, 1995), in addition to other, more informal, conversations.

2. Although he collected relatively little, Kroeber's colleague Pliny Goddard conducted important research among Klamath River peoples, particularly the Hupa and other Athapaskan-speakers. Goddard's *Life and Culture of the Hupa* (1903) contains much about carving. After Goddard's departure from Berkeley in 1909, Kroeber was assisted by Thomas T. Waterman. Waterman's fieldwork among the Yurok and Tolowa in the teens resulted in his classic *Yurok Geography* (1920), whose broad scope ranges much more widely than its title may suggest. Especially important in this context is its extensive coverage of villages, houses, and ownership. Undoubtedly, the most important of Kroeber's students to study Klamath River material culture was Lila O'Neale. She visited Hupa, Yurok, and Karuk basket weavers in 1929 to ask about their art, and her 1932 monograph is our best source on the aesthetics of these cultures. Philip Drucker's 1933 field trip enabled him to write the basic ethnography of the Tolowa (1937); in 1935, Harold Driver conducted fieldwork in order to compile an exhaustive list of cultural traits of the region (1939). Despite the valuable information recorded by these students, carving was treated only incidentally, and they did little collecting. One important scholar who was not part of the Berkeley circle was John P. Harrington, who worked as a linguist for the Smithsonian's Bureau of American Ethnology. Like Waterman's geographical study, his monograph on the use of tobacco among the Karuk (1932) includes a great deal of cultural context, including a substantial amount on carving.

3. The identity of Kroeber and Kelly's source is uncertain. He may have been the Robert Johnson, known as Orick Bob, who was one of Kroeber's Yurok informants and who also served as a caretaker of Kroeber's home near this community (T. Kroeber 1970:158). Or he may have been William Johnson of Rekwoi (Requa), a noted regalia maker (Kroeber 1976:437). Kelly says no more about him.

4. Other significant collections of carvings from the Klamath River area are the Grace Nicholson collections at the Smithsonian's National Museum of the American Indian (New York) and the Harvard Peabody Museum (Cambridge), the John Hudson collection at the Field Museum (Chicago), the Charles Wilcomb collection at the Oakland Museum (Oakland), the Southwest Museum

(Los Angeles), the California State Indian Museum (Sacramento), the Clarke Museum (Eureka), the Hoopa Tribal Museum (Hoopa), and the early (1793) Vancouver collection at the British Museum (London). While baskets from this region are common, large systematic collections of carved objects are relatively rare. Many museums, however, possess small numbers of elk antler spoons and purses.

5. Although he did not concentrate on the subject, Alfred Kroeber is our most comprehensive source for Klamath River material culture, especially in his *Handbook* chapter on Yurok arts (1925:76–97) and his informative set of comparative Yurok notes to Elmendorf's study of the Twana (Kroeber 1960). Completed just before his death, the latter study supercedes the *Handbook* version of Yurok culture on many points. Much of its information was compiled after Kroeber had gone over all his Yurok notes with Robert Spott in the 1930s and also after he had worked with colleagues like Edward Gifford and Samuel Barrett in the 1940s and 1950s.

6. Much more could be said about Klamath River house form and function; the following discussion gives only the most general information as a context for the carved elements of door, ladder, and furniture. For sources, see Goddard (1903:13–18), Thompson (1916:35–39), Kroeber (1925:78–82, 1960:150–170), Drucker (1937:235–36), Buckley (1987), Nabokov and Easton (1989:288–93).

7. As with the house, there is a large literature on Klamath River canoes; see Kroeber (1925:82–83; 1960:170–75, 182–92), Cunningham (1989:58–61), and Ortiz (1990).

8. This point is actually quite debated. For the argument against seagoing canoes, see Cunningham (1989:59). Jobson and Hildebrandt (1980) and Hudson (1981) support Gould, though in different ways.

9. Yurok women did use a plain digging stick for gathering clams, roots, and bulbs (Kroeber 1960:126).

10. According to Kroeber, "The *rumitsek* is a more or less globular basket in openwork, hung about the house to hold spoons, awls, sinews, and odds and ends. It is sometimes made very prettily with courses of crossed or gathered warp and a pleasingly equal mesh" (1925:91).

11. Kroeber observed examples of the venison trays in the University Museum still covered with deer grease. Goddard claimed that for religious purposes the Hupa never washed these (1903:23), but Kroeber was told that the Yurok custom was that they could be washed, but only in a basket of still water not in a stream (1960:136, 138). For more on Yurok eating customs see Kroeber (1960:137–38).

12. Kroeber noted, "Most ethnologically collected pipes that are wholly of steatite were made for sale to whites" (1960:246). However, he went on to note that "All-stone pipes may possibly have been made at times in the past, but the conservative Yurok point of view was that such were sacred and alive—like the historic one kept at Welkwau in connection with the First-Salmon ritual and perhaps a former Deerskin Dance—and that they ought therefore not be imitated profanely." As Beverly R. Ortiz commented (pers. comm.), one wonders how he reconciled these statements.

13. One kind of figurative sculpture has been found from archaeological remains in this region. Dating from around A.D. 1000 are animal effigy carvings of slate. Their use is unknown; they may have been wealth items or have been used for ceremonial killing of animals (Heizer and Elsasser 1980:188–89).

14. One possible exception to this generalization of skills was bow-making. Several scholars have noted specialized bow-makers (Mason 1889:228, Barrett 1961a:157).

15. This description, taken from Frank Gist, is confirmed by Samuel Barrett's journal. He noted that, according to Homer Cooper, only the base of the antler was used to make spoons; this forms the base of the spoon, the center of the antler being too cellular; the handle is made from the harder material along the sides. "He insists he has seen old men making these spoons from the base of the antler in this way and that that is the only part of the antler used for that purpose" (1960–62:51). Gist added, however, that on rare occasions spoons could be made from the upper branches of an antler. In that case, they would be very small and narrow.

16. On his first field trip to the Klamath River, Kroeber noted, "Deer horns used for spoons for acorn soup. Soaked, then carved. Elkhorn broken, pieces soaked, then rubbed on stone til [sic] became wedges" (Kroeber 1900:7). It is unclear if Kroeber ever observed this or if it was merely told to him.

17. It is not known if Klamath River peoples used a blue pigment before contact, and if so, what it may have been (Kroeber 1976:40).

18. Kroeber later went on to qualify this statement: "It would have been more exact to say that the names for the designs and patterns worked on baskets are the same as those applied to decorations on other objects: the subject was first approached from basketry, but the design names have no specific reference to baskets" (Kroeber and Barrett 1960:62).

19. In this passage, Kroeber's eliptic notes have been edited slightly for greater comprehension.

20. In an interesting aside, Kroeber observed that "actually a more interesting exhibit could be made if Yurok and perhaps preferably Karok were substituted for the Hupa, inasmuch as these tribes living off a reservation have

preserved more of the old life than the Hupa themselves." Expressing his archaic biases, he added, "A little weathering, or if necessary, smoking, would give these the genuine native flavor. There is also a greater wealth of house apparatus and utensils than in the other California cultures" (Kroeber 1931).

21. Cooper, George, and Moore would have been boys and young men when Kroeber came looking for "traditional" artifacts. Given the dramatic changes in Klamath River material culture at the time, one wonders how much opportunity they had to make elk antler spoons or sinew-backed bows.

22. A vivid example of Homer Cooper's teaching is the way he showed Blake how to make string: "I would be making a string for the bow, and he was telling me to spin it, and I said, 'spin it?' And then I went and I tried it, and I came back, and I was so frustrated. And when he showed me, he laid it in the palm of his hand, and he just took two batches, and he began to twist them with eighty-five year old knobby knuckles and feeble hands, and it was so easy, when I got the principle down. I just couldn't believe it, before my eyes, I could see string just emerging so easy and then I knew. But that's the way he taught me."

23. Two of Dewey George's ceremonial scenes, from 1968–69, are in the End of the Trail Indian Museum at the Trees of Mystery, a private park in Klamath, California. And there is another at the Clarke Museum in Eureka.

REFERENCES

Barrett, Samuel A. 1960–62. Journal. Accession no. 1994, ms. no. 55:13, 18–23, 50–52, 73–81. Phoebe Hearst Museum of Anthropology, University of California, Berkeley.

——. 1961a. American Indian Films. *Kroeber Anthropological Society Papers,* no. 25:155–62.

——. 1961b. *The Sinew-Backed Bow and Its Arrows.* Film, 16 mm., color, sound, 24 minutes. Berkeley: University of California Extension Media Center.

Barrett, Samuel A., Alfred L. Kroeber, and Thomas T. Waterman. ms. "Woodworking [of Northwestern California]." Accession no. 1983. Hearst Museum.

Batkin, Jonathan. 1987. Pottery: The Ceramic Tradition. In *Harmony By Hand: Art of the Southwest Indians,* by Patrick Houlihan, Jerold L. Collings, Sarah Nestor, and Jonathan Batkin, 77–103. San Francisco: Chronicle Books.

Blackman, Margaret B. 1976. Creativity in Acculturation: Art, Architecture, and Ceremony from the Northwest Coast. *Ethnohistory* 23(4):387–413.

Blackman, Margaret B., and Edwin S. Hall, Jr. 1982. The After Image and Image After: Visual Documents and the Renaissance in Northwest Coast Art. *American Indian Art Magazine* 7(2):30–39.

Bright, William. 1978. Karok. In *California,* ed. Robert F. Heizer. *Handbook of North American Indians,* ed. William C. Sturtevant, 8:180–89. Washington, D.C.: Smithsonian Institution.

Buckley, Thomas. 1987. Yurok Houses. *News from Native California* 1(3):10–11.

Bushnell, John H. 1968. From American Indian to Indian American: The Changing Identity of the Hupa. *American Anthropologist* 70:1108–16.

Buzaljko, Grace Wilson. 1993. Isabel Kelly: From Museum Anthropologist to Archaeologist. In *Museum Anthropology in California,* 1889–1939, eds. Ira Jacknis and Margot Blum Schevill. *Museum Anthropology* 17(2):41–48.

Collier, Mary E. T., and Sylvia Barker Thalman, eds. 1991. *Interviews with Tom Smith and Maria Copa: Isabel Kelly's Ethnographic Notes on the Coast Miwok Indians of Marin and Southern Sonoma Counties, California.* MAPOM Occasional Papers, no. 6. San Rafael, Cal.: Miwok Archeological Preserve of Marin.

Conn, Richard. 1979. *Native American Art in the Denver Art Museum.* Denver: Denver Art Museum.

Cunningham, Richard W. 1989. *California Indian Watercraft.* San Luis Obispo: EZ Nature Books.

Curtis, Edward S. 1924. Hupa, Yurok, Karok, Wiyot, Tolowa and Tututni, Shasta, Achomawi, Klamath. *The North American Indian,* 13. Norwood, Mass.: Plimpton Press.

Driver, Harold E. 1939. *Culture Element Distributions: X, Northwest California.* Anthropological Records, 1(6):297–433. Berkeley and Los Angeles: University of California Press.

Drucker, Philip. 1937. *The Tolowa and their Southwest Oregon Kin.* University of California Publications in American Archaeology and Ethnology, 36(4):221–300. Berkeley: University of California Press.

Elsasser, Albert B. 1978. Wiyot. In *California,* ed. Robert F. Heizer. *Handbook of North American Indians,* ed. William C. Sturtevant, 8:180–89. Washington, D.C.: Smithsonian Institution.

Elsasser, Albert B., and Robert F. Heizer. 1966. *Excavation of Two Northwestern California Coastal Sites.* Reports of the University of California Archaelogical Survey, no. 67. Berkeley: University of California Archaeological Research Facility.

Frank, Weitchpec. [1901?]. Yurok Notebook, no. 15, A. L. Kroeber papers, carton 6, The Bancroft Library, University of California, Berkeley.

Frederickson, David A. 1984. The North Coastal Region. In *California Archaeology,* by Michael J. Moratto, 471–527. Orlando: Academic Press.

Goddard, Pliny E. 1903. *Life and Culture of the Hupa.* University of California Publications in American Archaeology and Ethnology, 1(1):1–88. Berkeley: University of California Press.

Gould, Richard A. 1968. Seagoing Canoes among the Indians of Northwestern California. *Ethnohistory* 15(1):11–42.

——. 1978. Tolowa. In *California,* ed. Robert F. Heizer. *Handbook of North American Indians,* ed. William C. Sturtevant, 8:128–36. Washington, D.C.: Smithsonian Institution.

Harrington, John P. 1932. *Tobacco Among the Karuk Indians of California.* Bureau of American Ethnology Bulletin, no. 94. Washington, D.C.: Smithsonian Institution.

Heizer, Robert F., and Albert B. Elsasser. 1980. *The Natural World of the California Indians.* Berkeley and Los Angeles: University of California Press.

Heizer, Robert F., and John E. Mills. 1952. *The Four Ages of Tsurai: A Documentary History of the Indian Village on Trinidad Bay.* Berkeley and Los Angeles: University of California Press.

Hudson, Travis. 1981. To Sea or Not to Sea: Further Notes on the "Oceangoing" Dugouts of North Coastal California. *Journal of California and Great Basin Anthropology* 3(2):269–82.

Jacknis, Ira. 1991. California. In *Objects of Myth and Memory: American Indian Art at The Brooklyn Museum,* by Diana Fane, Ira Jacknis, and Lise M. Breen, 161–231. Brooklyn: The Brooklyn Museum/Seattle: University of Washington Press.

——. 1993. Alfred Kroeber as Museum Anthropologist. In *Museum Anthropology in California, 1889–1939,* eds. Ira Jacknis and Margot Blum Schevill. *Museum Anthropology* 17(2):27–32.

——. 1994. Introduction. In *Indian Regalia of Northwest California,* 2–4. Berkeley: Phoebe Hearst Museum of Anthropology.

Jobson, Robert W., and William R. Hildebrandt. 1980. The Distribution of Oceangoing Canoes on the North Coast of California. *Journal of California and Great Basin Anthropology* 2(2):165–74.

Johnson, Mark, Moira Roth, and Diane Tani, eds. 1992. *Brian D. Tripp.* Berkeley: Visibility Press/Berkeley Store Gallery.

Jones, Philip Mills. 1901. Diary, entry for July 27. Accession no. 19. Hearst Museum.

Kelly, Isabel T. 1930a. *Peruvian Cumbrous Bowls.* University of California Publications in American Archaeology and Ethnology, 24(6):325–41. Berkeley: University of California Press.

——. 1930b. *The Carver's Art of the Indians of Northwestern California.* University of California Publications in American Archaeology and Ethnology, 24(7):343–60. Berkeley: University of California Press.

——. 1930c. *Yuki Basketry.* University of California Publications in American Archaeology and Ethnology, 24(9):421–44. Berkeley: University of California Press.

Knobloch, Patricia J. 1988. Isabel Truesdell Kelly. In *Women Anthropologists: A Biographical Dictionary,* eds. Ute Gacs, Aisha Khan, Jerrie McIntyre, Ruth Weinberg, 175–80. Westport, Conn.: Greenwood Press.

Kroeber, Alfred L. [1900]. Yurok Notebook, no. 2, A. L. Kroeber papers, The Bancroft Library.

——. 1905. *Basket Designs of the Indians of Northwestern California.* University of California Publications in American Archaeology and Ethnology, 2(4):105–64. Berkeley: University of California Press.

——. 1925. *Handbook of the Indians of California.* Bureau of American Ethnology Bulletin, no. 78. Washington, D.C.: Smithsonian Institution.

——. 1931. Letter to Edward W. Gifford, October 31; Folder: Museum History: Museum of Anthropology, 1931; Hearst Museum.

——. 1960 [1992]. Comparative Notes on the Structure of Yurok Culture. In *The Structure of Twana Culture*, by William W. Elmendorf. Reprint ed. Pullman: Washington State University Press.

——. 1976. *Yurok Myths*. Berkeley and Los Angeles: University of California Press.

Kroeber, Alfred L., and Samuel A. Barrett. 1960. *Fishing Among the Indians of Northwestern California*. Anthropological Records, 21(1):1–210. Berkeley and Los Angeles: University of California Press.

Kroeber, Alfred L., and Edward W. Gifford. 1980. *Karok Myths*. Berkeley and Los Angeles: University of California Press.

Kroeber, Theodora. 1970. *Alfred Kroeber: A Personal Configuration*. Berkeley and Los Angeles: University of California Press.

LaPena, Frank R., and Janice T. Driesbach, eds. 1985. *The Extension of Tradition: Contemporary Northern California Native American Art in Cultural Perspective*. Sacramento: Crocker Museum of Art.

Mason, Otis T. 1889. The Ray Collection from Hupa Reservation. In *Annual Report of the Smithsonian Institution for 1886*, pt. 1:205–39. Washington, D.C.

Nabokov, Peter, and Robert Easton. 1989. *Native American Architecture*. New York: Oxford University Press.

O'Neale, Lila M. 1932. *Yurok-Karok Basket Weavers*. University of California Publications in American Archaeology and Ethnology, 32(1):1–184. Berkeley: University of California Press.

Ortiz, Bev. 1990. A Rich Red Hue: Yurok Dugout Canoes. *News from Native California* 5(1):12–16.

——. 1994. A Commitment to the Future: The Artistry of Frank Gist. *News from Native California* 7(4):17–20.

——. 1995. George Blake: A Traditional/Contemporary Artist. *News from Native California* 8(4):30–34.

Parkman, E. Breck. 1987. Building a Yurok Village. *News from Native California* 1(3):8–10.

——. 1991. Dedicating Sumeg. *News from Native California* 5(2):4–8.

Petersen, David. 1988. *Among the Elk: Wilderness Images*. Flagstaff: Northland Press.

Pilling, Arnold R. 1978. Yurok. In *California*, ed. Robert F. Heizer. *Handbook of North American Indians*, ed. William C. Sturtevant, 8:137–54. Washington, D.C.: Smithsonian Institution.

——. 1989. Yurok Aristocracy and "Great Houses." *The American Indian Quarterly* 13(4):421–36.

Powers, Stephen. 1877 [1976]. *Tribes of California,* Introduction and annotations by Robert F. Heizer. Reprint ed. Berkeley and Los Angeles: University of California Press.

Schenck, Sara M., and Edward W. Gifford. 1952. *Karok Ethnobotany.* Anthropological Records, 13(6):377–92. Berkeley and Los Angeles: University of California Press.

Smith-Ferri, Sherrie. 1993. Basket Weavers, Basket Collectors, and the Market: A Case Study of Joseppa Dick. In *Museum Anthropology in California, 1889–1939,* eds. Ira Jacknis and Margot Blum Schevill. *Museum Anthropology* 17(2):61–66.

Spott, Robert. 1939. Folder: "Yurok Notes—Reality Culture," A. L. Kroeber papers, carton 7, The Bancroft Library.

Steiner, Christopher B. 1994. *African Art in Transit.* Cambridge: Cambridge University Press.

Thompson, Lucy. 1916 [1991]. *To the American Indian: Reminiscences of a Yurok Woman.* Reprint ed. Berkeley: Heyday Books.

Thoresen, Timothy H. H. 1976. Kroeber and the Yurok, 1900–1908. In *Yurok Myths,* Alfred Kroeber, xix–xxviii. Berkeley and Los Angeles: University of California Press.

Wallace, William J. 1978. Hupa, Chilula, and Whilkut. In *California,* ed. Robert F. Heizer. *Handbook of North American Indians,* ed. William C. Sturtevant, 8:164–79. Washington, D.C.: Smithsonian Institution.

Wasserman, Abby. 1986. R. E. Bartow. In *Portfolio: Eleven American Indian Artists.* San Francisco: American Indian Contemporary Arts.

Waterman, Thomas T. 1920. *Yurok Geography.* University of California Publications in American Archaeology and Ethnology, 16(5):177–314. Berkeley: University of California Press.

THE CARVER'S ART OF THE INDIANS OF NORTHWESTERN CALIFORNIA

by Isabel T. Kelly

University of California Publications in
American Archaeology and Ethnology
Volume 24, No. 7, pp. 343–360, plates 103–119, 7 figures in text
Issued August 6, 1930

University of California Press
Berkeley, California

Cambridge University Press
London, England

THE CARVER'S ART OF THE INDIANS OF NORTHWESTERN CALIFORNIA

BY

ISABEL T. KELLY

CONTENTS

LIST OF PLATES

(Following page 360)

FIGURES IN TEXT

The Indians of northwestern California occupy a peculiar place in cultural schemes. Although they exhibit a number of typical California traits (such as the mush paddle, lack of symbolism), the preponderance of evidence indicates northern affiliation, and they are usually reckoned as the southern outpost of the North Pacific coast culture area. Aside from northern and southern importations, this area is characterized by certain local developments—the stool, the pillow, the mush paddle, and the horn purse and spoon. The group is definitely intermediate in culture and yet far from parasitic.

The typical tribes of this area are the Yurok, Karok, and Hupa, living along the lower Klamath and Trinity rivers. The Karok and

Hupa are inland; the Yurok extend to and along the coast. Although unrelated linguistically,[1] these three tribes are almost identical in culture.

The principal art is carving in wood and horn. The wooden head-rest, canoe prow, and stool, are nicely shaped, although they rarely bear designs (Goddard, fig. 1,[2] and Kroeber, pls. 15 and 19).[3] However, these articles are characterized by a high degree of skill in execution and finish and attest the excellence of the carver's art. The plank which serves as house entrance is often decorated, sometimes with a row of dots around the door, or triangles carved above (pl. 118*a*, and Waterman, pl. 4).[4]

The principal objects decorated are the horn spoon, the wooden mush stirrer, the horn purse, and to a minor extent such articles as bone hairpins, head-scratchers, horn mesh sticks, and dentalium shells (pl. 119).

HORN SPOONS

Carved spoons are manufactured from elk horn and occasionally from deer horn and wood. Deer horn is harder than elk horn, and the spoons are smaller and less elaborate. The wooden spoons show a slight tendency toward curvilinear outline, owing doubtless to the more easily worked medium, but ordinarily all spoons adhere to the same general pattern.

We have no definite description of the manufacture of spoons. It is said that in the old days the horn was soaked until soft and the spoon then shaped by rubbing with sandstone. Only the horn near the base of the antler was used.[5] The bowl was made from the thickened cross-section and the handle from the adjacent vertical horn. If this is true, the stem-bowl angle is obtained naturally and not by heating and bending, as among the Kwakiutl.[6] The latter also claim rubbing with sandstone to be the aboriginal method. An examination of the spoons under a magnifying glass reveals the undoubted use of a sharp instrument on most of the elaborate specimens, although the polish tends to obscure the means of shaping. It is quite probable

---

1 The Yurok are Algonkin; the Hupa, Athapascan; and the Karok, Hokan.

2 Goddard, Life and Culture of the Hupa, UC–PAAE, 1:1–88, 1903.

3 Kroeber, Handbook of the Indians of California, BAE–B, 78, 1925.

4 Waterman, Yurok Geography, UC–PAAE, 16:177–314, 1920.

5 These statements are upon the authority of Mr. Robert Johnson, a Yurok, in conversation with Dr. Kroeber.

6 Boas, Franz, Ethnology of the Kwakiutl, BAE–R, 35, part 1:104, 1921.

that these were made after the adoption of modern tools. Some twenty spoons have a hole for hanging. Four of these holes have been made by drilling from one side and then from the other, leaving a ridge in the center. This is the old method of drilling. More frequently the hole seems to have been made by rubbing until the horn was thin enough to be pierced with a sharp instrument. The edges of the holes are still quite jagged. There is but one case which suggests the use of the gimlet.

The carved spoons were used by the men. Women used a mussel shell, a piece of deer skull, or a piece of undecorated elk horn of "shoe-horn" shape (pls. 105*a* and 119*b*). The men's spoons are shaped much like our modern spoons. The handle meets the bowl at a 45° angle, but occasionally approaches 90°. The upper part of the handle is usually sprung back, probably by the use of heat.

The height of the spoons ranges from 15 to 22 cm. and the width of the bowl from 5 to 7 cm. The bowl is usually longer than wide; it may be almost flat or may be well rounded. The rounding may be increased artificially as the sweep of the bowl is often considerable.

The shape of the spoons adheres fairly constantly to a definite structural pattern. The elements, exclusive of the bowl, may be likened to a column—at the base a pedestal, above it a stem, and at the top a capital. This parallel will provide a convenient terminology. Of the one hundred eight horn spoons, only three lack a capital, and only twelve a pedestal. None of the finished spoons lack both.

The capitals fall into three groups according to outline—the round, the rectangular, and the beehive. The latter group, having a rounded top and a rectangular base, is intermediate between the rectangular and the round. The beehive type is the most numerous, with the round next. This grouping accounts for practically every specimen. The only difficulty lies in differentiating between the three types: a capital may be somewhat rounded at the corners and yet appear essentially quadrilateral.

The capitals vary in width from 10 to 28 mm., with 60 per cent falling between 16 and 24 mm. The mean is 19 mm. These calculations are based on the eighty-five of the one hundred eight specimens which lent themselves to measurement. In height, the range is from 8 to 26 mm. with a mean of 17 mm. Seventy per cent of the cases fall between 13 and 21 mm. The height of sixty-three capitals was measured. The ratio procured by dividing the width by the height runs from sixty to two hundred seventy-five with the mean at one hundred nineteen. Twenty-six cases, or 43 per cent of the sixty-one measured, are from 1 to 1.19 times as wide as high.

The pedestal is likewise a constant feature. Its origin is problematical. There is no indication that it strengthens the spoon, but it serves nicely as a transition between the wide bowl and the narrow stem.

Ninety-six of the one hundred eight specimens have a definitely recognizable pedestal. These are of two principal types—quadrilateral and inverted funnel. In the latter case, of which there are thirty-two instances, the sides of the pedestal converge and run into the stem. Obviously this is no more than a plain spoon notched at the top of the bowl.

The quadrilateral pedestals range from rectangular to trapezoidal in outline. A two-millimeter difference in width at the top and base gives a noticeable slant. Where the difference is less than 2 mm., or where the disparity seems attributable to inaccuracy rather than intention, the pedestal is not ranked as trapezoidal. Some show variation as great as 12 mm., but most range from 2 to 6. The transition from bowl to stem is doubtless responsible for the slanting line, as the trapezoidal form is practically lacking in capitals. Only six of the capitals measured show a difference of more than one millimeter between top and bottom, and none of more than 3 mm.

The pedestals vary in width from 14 to 42 mm. with 29 mm. as the mean and 28 mm. as the mode. This is based on eighty-one cases. The height ranges from 4 to 29 mm. with a mean of 12 mm. About 43 per cent of the fifty-six cases are between 8 and 12 mm. It is impossible to measure the height of the funnel pedestal, as there is no break at the stem. In no case does the height of the pedestal exceed the width. The ratios range from one hundred to six hundred eighty-three, with a mean of two hundred eighty-two. Fifty-three per cent of the pedestals are from 1.80 to 3.29 times as wide as high. This tendency is scarcely perceptible in the capitals where the height frequently exceeds the width. The pedestal is far wider than the capital both proportionately and absolutely. The proximity of the bowl is undoubtedly the causal factor.

Calculations based on measurement of eighty cases give + .49 for the correlation between the greatest width of the capital and the greatest width of the pedestal. The data for the respective heights are fewer, since it is impossible to gauge the height of the funnel pedestals; but on the basis of forty-nine specimens, a correlation coefficient of .38 was obtained. There is obviously a stronger relation between the respective widths than between the heights; .49 is not a particularly high figure, but it may be regarded as reasonably significant.

There seems to be no particular association between any type of capital and any type of pedestal. The combination of any two types is about as frequent as chance expectation would have it.

A classification of spoons may be approximated along the following lines:

1. *Plain spoons.*—These spoons have shaped bowls and handles but are devoid of the usual decorative features. All the twenty-three specimens have capitals, and each type of capital is represented. Seven have no pedestal; the normal expectancy would be but two. The remainder of the spoons have either funnel or quadrilateral pedestals. Nineteen are Yurok; three, Hupa; and one of doubtful provenience. However, this fact is of no especial significance, as 70 per cent of the entire collection is Yurok, and the remainder is Hupa.

2. *Spoons undecorated but for notches.*—These spoons would come under the previous classification but for the notching. All but one have the pedestal notched; several have the stem or capital also marked. Fourteen of the sixteen have quadrilateral pedestals. The normal expectancy would be eight. No particular type of capital predominates. Thirteen are Yurok, two are Hupa, and one is of doubtful source.

3. *Spoons with zigzag handles.*—Two principal types of zigzag are represented. The first obtains the effect by the stepped superimposition of parallelograms. The sides slant toward the left. This is a popular basketry motif but occurs only twice in the spoons. The other type is the familiar right-angle or obtuse-angle zigzag, of which there are fourteen cases. Six are Hupa, seven are Yurok, and one is doubtful. The number of angles varies from one to five on a side. In six instances both sides bear the same number of angles; in six instances the right side (as one faces the spoon) has one more angle than the left. Only two instances of the converse occur. This type of spoon seems not to be associated with any particular type of capital or pedestal. Notching is frequent, especially on the pedestal.

4. *Spoons with trapezoid, lozenge, or hourglass handles.*—This series of designs may easily have originated from the funnel element, and the supposition is strengthened by the absence of the trapezoid on

purse engravings. The diamond and hourglass are found there, but in that instance are the outgrowth of triangle combinations.

Notches placed at the top of the bowl produce a funnel pedestal. By repeating the notching up the handle, a series of superimposed trapezoids is formed. This tiered handle is the most common, occurring in fifteen of the twenty-nine spoons. Pleasing variation is obtained by inverting the series halfway up the handle. The tiered handle is usually associated with the funnel pedestal, although the quadrilateral is frequent. It may have any kind of capital.

If the funnel motif be inverted, an hourglass figure is formed. By repeated alternate inversions, two hourglass figures, or a diamond flanked on either end by a trapezoid, are automatically produced. Because of this, it is sometimes uncertain whether the design is a diamond or an hourglass (pl. 107*c*).

There are two kinds of diamond-shaped stems. With one, the stem converges at the capital and pedestal, making the whole shaft a single lozenge. The diamond thus formed is usually notched at its lateral apices, dividing the stem into two long, funnel-shaped figures with bases touching. More commonly the stem is carved into a series of diamonds.

5. *Openwork spoons.*—Some 20 per cent of the spoons have openwork decoration. Where this overlaps with the trapezoid-lozenge heading the specimens are counted both ways. The openwork tends to take the form of one, two, or three longitudinal slits down the stem (eighteen out of twenty-two cases). Other times small diamond or triangular pieces have been removed, leaving a zigzag outline.

All but seven spoons fall into the foregoing five classes. Six of these seven are barred from the second class only because of incising. The seventh spoon is quite anomalous.

Decoration is not confined to the stem outline. Relief work, notching, and incising are used. The first is rare. Notching is found on forty-eight spoons. Occasionally imitation notching is made by small incisions along the edges. Notching occurs twenty times on the pedestal alone, and nine times on the pedestal and stem. It appears less frequently in other combinations. The incising is not particularly noteworthy. There are five cases of imitation notching, four of a row of short, transverse lines down the back of the stem, three of incised dots, three of crosses, and six of horizontal or diagonal lines. The zigzag appears once in incising. As a general thing, engraving on the spoons is inferior work.

The surface of fully one-third of the capitals is depressed. This may have been suggested by the natural curve of the horn, but is frequently found where there is no trace of concavity on the stem. The face seems to have been rubbed until the desired hollow was produced. This depression is usually associated with a round or beehive capital.

About the same number of spoons have a bevel or ridge. This is usually down the back of the stem or on the back of the pedestal and upper part of the bowl. It occurs three times on the face of the handle. This is a definitely strengthening feature, perhaps suggested by the contour of the horn.

In general, the spoons adhere to a structural pattern—capital, stem, pedestal, and bowl. The capital, pedestal, and stem are worked into characteristic designs. There is no evidence that the decoration of any one part is associated with that of any other part. There is no indication of tribal differentiation. This collection is attributed, 70 per cent to the Yurok, with 30 per cent Hupa. However, the source of manufacture was not ascertained by collectors, and some pieces may have been acquired by their owners in trade, so that the Karok and Tolowa may be represented in the collection.

Aesthetically, the cream of the lot is represented by some thirty-five spoons, elaborately carved and nicely polished. In these, there is a noticeable preference for symmetry in shape and decoration, but an apparent disregard of accuracy in detail. Sixteen of these specimens are rather elaborately carved but show minor discrepancies in the number of notches and the like. The zigzag, if not exactly symmetrical, gives a satisfactory sense of balance. There seems to be no repetition of a certain, preferred number in the decoration; five and ten, the ritual numbers, do not occur more frequently than others. There is nothing to indicate that the carving is other than merely decorative.

MUSH PADDLES

A paddle is used to stir the hot stones in boiling mush. Most of the blades are charred from use. The paddles are of hard wood, from two to four feet in height. The paddle-like stirrer is found widely spread in California, as far south as the Diegueño, but is usually undecorated, except among the northwestern tribes, where it is nicely carved.[7]

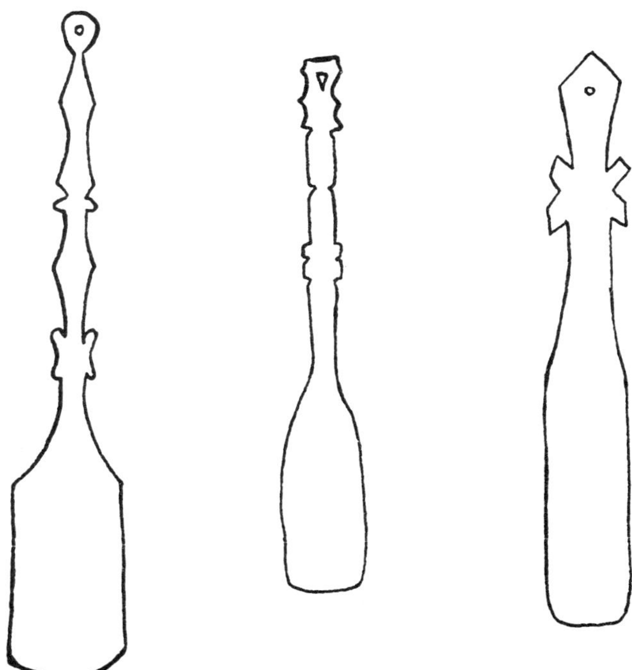

Fig. 1. Iroquois food paddles, strikingly similar to those of northwestern California, even to identical design units. After Waugh.

The paddle is best described by comparison with the spoon. It is immediately apparent that the stirrer follows the capital, stem, and pedestal pattern. The blade is comparable to the bowl, but is flat and much elongated. Eight of the fifty-four paddles are without capitals. Round, beehive, and rectangular capitals are all represented, the first

[7] Although typical of California, the mush paddle is by no means confined to this area. It is found among the Thompson (Teit, The Thompson Indians of British Columbia, AMNH–M, 2:203, 1900) and is mentioned for the Menomini (Skinner, Material Culture of the Menomini, MAIHF–INM, 148, 166, 170, 1921). The Iroquois implement is strikingly similar in shape and decoration (Waugh, Iroquois foods and food preparation, Canada Geological Survey, Memoir 86:70, pls. 29, 30, 70, 1916). Three of these implements are reproduced in figure 1 of this paper.

by five, the second by four, and the last by eleven cases. Several new types of capital are also found. The trapezoid, probably a variation of the rectangular, is prominent with eleven cases. Its slanting sides may be less likely to split than those of the rectangular, which would follow the grain of the wood. A number of diverse outlines have been included in a cylindrical group, which is composed of those capitals in

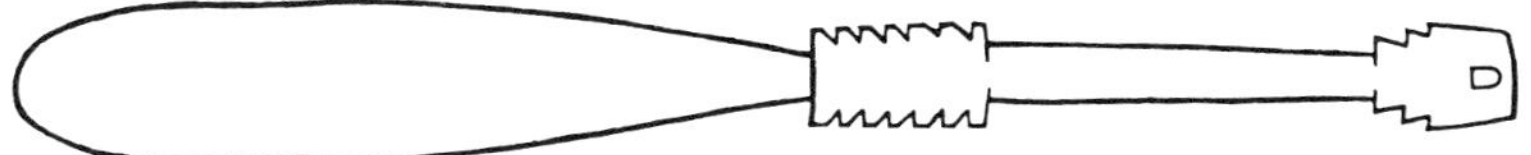

Fig. 2. Wooden paddle.

which the third dimension could not be ignored. Should one disregard this element and consider outline alone, these capitals would fall under the other headings. Six would be rectangular, one round, two beehive, five trapezoid, and one anomalous.

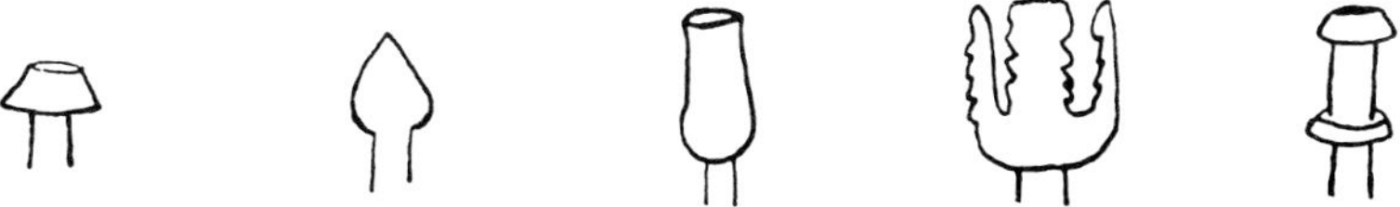

Fig. 3. Cylindrical capitals of mush paddles.

The capitals, measured at their point of greatest width, vary from 20 to 84 mm. with a mean of 46 mm. The height runs from 13 to 122 mm. with the mean at 50 mm. The capital is from .31 to 2.72 times as wide as high. The greatest number of cases lie between .90 and 1.09; the mean is 1.10. The ratio is somewhat smaller than for the spoons; that is, paddle capitals are narrower.

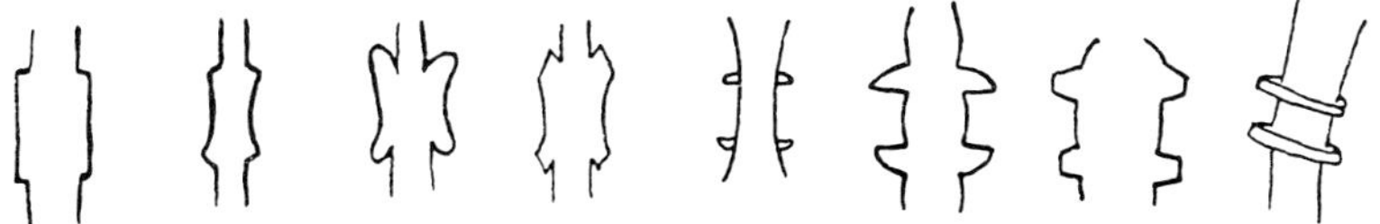

Fig. 4. Modified rectangular pedestals of mush paddles.

Only two paddles are without a pedestal. There are four funnel, one round, three anomalous, and six cylindrical pedestals. The latter would all be rectangular were outline the sole criterion. There are no trapezoidal pedestals. The rectangle is the most common, with thirty-eight occurrences. It is shown above, with some of its modifications.

The pedestals measure 36 to 103 mm. at their widest point. The mean is 60 mm. The height varies from 27 to 250 mm. with the mean at 91 mm. In striking contrast to the spoons, the pedestal tends to be taller than wide. The ratios run from sixteen to two hundred six with 57 per cent between forty and sixty-nine. The mean of the ratios is seventy-three. This difference in proportion is to be expected. The paddle is essentially a long, flat implement whose width could be contained in two slightly converging lines enclosing the pedestal and blade at their points of greatest width. It tends to length rather than to width. With the spoons, the situation is quite different. The pedestal, intermediate between the stem and the bowl, must inevitably have been influenced by the width of the latter. This comes out clearly in the correlation figures for the widths of the respective capitals and pedestals. The paddle measurements give .70, a rather high figure. The spoon correlation of .49 is indicative of reasonable relationship, but has undoubtedly been lowered by the contiguity of the bowl. This influence is lacking in the paddle, where the pedestal is sometimes the widest part. The correlation between the greatest height of the capital and of the pedestal is only .16 for the paddle, but .38 for the spoon.

The paddle may be compared to the spoon in several other elements of shape. In the first place, the spoon handle is usually flat, while that of the paddle may be rounded or even cylindrical. This element of third dimension has undoubtedly encouraged the variety of capital and pedestal decoration. In the second place, the capital of the paddles is never depressed. This furthers the belief that the hollow of the spoon capital developed from the curve of the horn. A bevel, frequent in spoons, occurs but five times. This suggests that its use in the spoons is purely a matter of reinforcement. About the same proportion of paddles as of spoons is pierced for hanging. There is no indication that the hole in paddles is associated with the round capital.

The paddle and spoon differ more fundamentally in decoration than in shape. The stirrer, unlike the spoon, indulges in elaboration of capital and pedestal rather than in stem decoration. Thirty-nine of the fifty-four paddles have smooth handles, but many modifications of the basic capital and pedestal shapes are found. More specific differences are found in the use of design elements. For example, in paddle decoration the trapezoid is confined largely to the capital. With the spoon it is used either as a pedestal or in combination to form a tiered handle. A further example is supplied by the hourglass motif. With the spoons this occurs frequently as an element of stem decoration, but almost never as a capital or pedestal. The converse is true of the paddle, where the hourglass is not used on the stem but is the most common pedestal shape (50 per cent of all the paddles). It also occurs occasionally as a capital.

Further comparison reveals an almost total absence of the zigzag on paddles. There are only two specimens, one of which appears to be of the superimposed parallelogram type. The zigzag does not appear in the engraving and only once in the openwork.

The openwork is about half as frequent as in spoons. With the latter it usually takes the form of longitudinal slits down the stem, but this is not characteristic of such openwork as is found in the paddles.

Relief work is rare enough in the paddles, but even then is more frequent than in the spoons. It usually involves the overlapping of the pedestal and blade (pl. 110*e*). Most of the relief work is very pleasing.

Over 20 per cent (twelve cases) of the paddles have some sort of engraved decoration. The principal characters include the triangle, cross, diamond, and straight and diagonal lines. Some of the incising is quite elaborate, at least in comparison with that of the spoons. About half the cases show a concentric motif. Although notching is tremendously popular as a spoon decoration, especially in pedestals, it occurs but seven times in the paddles and then is usually on the capital.

In general, the spoons and paddles differ more noticeably in decoration than in shape. Some of these differences (such as incising, notching, and relief work) can be satisfactorily explained by the natural potentialities of the two materials. Obviously, notching would be unsatisfactory in wood, as the soft material would tend to splinter. The absence or presence of certain design motives seems to be more arbitrary, but, regardless of such minor diversities, the spoon and the paddle give one a very definite impression of affinity.

ELK-HORN MONEY BOXES

The money box is an invention peculiar to northwestern California and is a corollary of the economic and social stress laid on wealth. It is usually of elk (but occasionally of deer) antler and has two principal shapes. The first is made from the fork of the antler (pl. 117, *k*, *l*). There are only three such specimens in the collection, and none of them show anything distinctive in the way of decoration.

The second type of purse is cylindrical but follows the curve of the horn. It is from 75 to 125 mm. in length. The concave face is slit and the porous inner material removed. The spongy part may be left at the ends and covered with pitch or paint. In one instance it has been replaced by a wooden plug.

The cylindrical box adheres to a structural pattern as constant as that of the spoons and paddles. The middle part of the box is worked down, leaving an enlargement on either end. This raised ring or flange provides support for the lid and strengthens the whole container. Thirty-eight of the fifty-three cylindrical purses[8] are shaped this way, and in eleven others the end treatment is indicated by the decoration. Only four purses show no trace of the pattern.

The opening is covered by a splint, often the same piece which was sliced off to make the slot. Many of the purses lack this lid and according to Goddard[9] are incomplete. Frequently crevices are cut in the flanges so that the lid can be sprung in snugly. The cover may be further secured by a thong wrapping (pl. 117).

Ten of the purses have small projections at each end (pls. 113*c*, 114*b*). Their use is unknown, but they may have been for carrying.[10]

The transverse groove (pl. 115*a*, *b*, *c*) is the most popular form of decoration. The most frequent incised designs are the triangle and the zigzag. In fourteen cases it is impossible to tell which of the two is intended. Right-angle triangles are often arranged in a double row so as to form a zigzag of bisected parallelograms (pl. 117*c*). Both this and the normal type of zigzag (pl. 115*a*) occur.

Barring grooves, the acute isosceles triangle is the most popular design element. It occurs on twenty-six of the thirty-one incised specimens. The obtuse triangle occurs four times. About the same proportion holds for those indeterminate as triangles or zigzags. The right-angle triangle occurs seven times, the hourglass twice, the diamond and cross-hatching three times each. The diamond and hourglass occur as separate entities, but in several instances are formed by triangle combinations. Incised dots occur five times. The trapezoid is completely lacking.

The designs are usually arranged in transverse or longitudinal rows. Oblique decoration occurs three times. The design area cen-

[8] Two of these 53 are attributed to the Modoc, 7 to the Hupa, and the balance to the Yurok.

[9] UC–PAAE, 1:49, 1903.

[10] The dance basket is fashioned on the same pattern as the purse, even to the projections on either end, Kroeber, UC–PAAE, 2: pl. 18, 1905.

ters around two structural features, the slit and the transverse end enlargements. The latter are usually banded by transverse grooves, and further decorated by one or more rows of triangles. A transverse arrangement of design does not occur except on the ends. Decoration of the longitudinal body is usually longitudinal, and rows of triangles frequently frame the opening. The acute triangle is the most common (sixteen out of twenty cases). The obtuse and the right-angle triangle occur three times each. Straight lines or rows of triangles occasionally run obliquely from the opening (pl. 114*a*). The back or sides may bear longitudinal rows of triangles, diamonds, or zigzags.

The lid and projections from the ends are sometimes incised. The usual straight line, triangle, diamond, and hourgless motives are found. The lid design matches that of the box in two cases, but, in general, there seems to be no necessary correspondence between the two.

The incisions are darkened and show up well against the natural cream or tawny background. Red, black, or blue paint may be rubbed in the grooves or applied to the porous ends. The use of colored pigment is noteworthy, as it is conspicuously absent from the spoons and paddles.

In general, the decoration tends to be symmetrical, particularly in the number of grooves at the ends. Three is the most common number of grooves, but inaccuracy in detail is apparent here as with the spoons. A row short one or two triangles was apparently no cause for concern. The designs are usually made solid, but there is slight tendency to do this by concentric filling.

CYLINDRICAL BOXES

The large wooden box in which dance regalia are stored follows the horn purse pattern closely. It has the same enlarged ends and occasionally the transverse grooves. Other than this the boxes are seldom decorated. One shown in plate 118*c* has a carved zigzag motif. The boxes are usually cylindrical[11] although there is one rectangular box in the Museum.

[11] Kroeber, BAE–B 78:92, 1925.

OTHER INCISED ARTICLES

Minor articles, such as bone hairpins, head-scratchers, dentalium shells, and elk-horn mesh sticks are occasionally incised (pl. 119). The designs are in keeping with those of the purses and consist of triangles, zigzags, and straight lines. The mesh sticks are usually

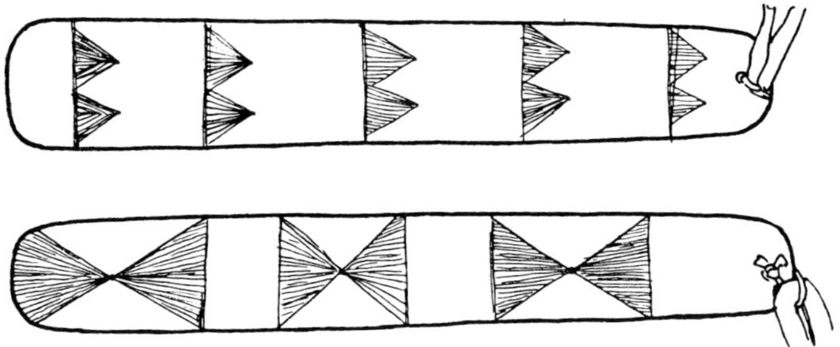

Fig. 5. Head-scratchers with incised triangular designs. Specimen nos. 1–1245a, 1–1246.

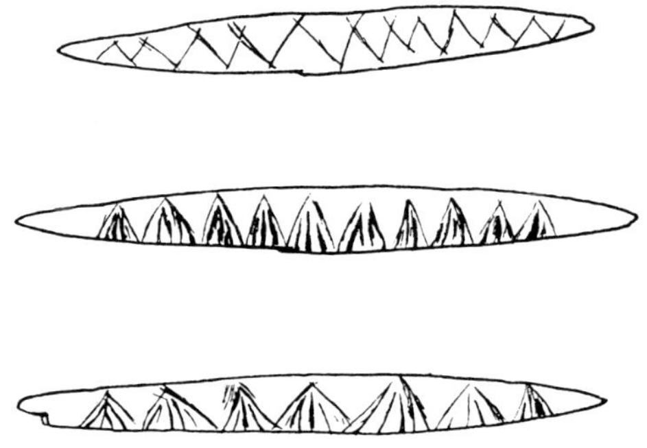

Fig. 6. Incised hairpins. Specimen nos. 1–2190, 1–2189, 1–2191.

decorated with plain lines, but this may be mere coincidence. A stone club[12] has a single zigzag engraved on its face. This is the only indication of incising on stone. In general, this minor incising is what one would expect after observation of the purses.

---

[12] Loud, Ethnogeography and Archaeology of the Wiyot Territory, UC–PAAE, 14: pl. 18, 1918.

RELATION OF CARVING TO BASKETRY DESIGNS[13]

In general, basketry designs are disposed horizontally below the rim, in contrast to the vertical field of the paddle, spoon, and to some extent the purse. Aside from this consideration the two arts differ moderately.

Certain of the familiar carving designs are lacking or but feebly represented in basketry. The hourglass occurs once as a modified snake-nose design, but seems to be rare. The trapezoid, as such, seems to be lacking, at least it is not figured in Kroeber's paper on basketry. Goddard[14] illustrates his discussion of technique by a sketch of a truncated triangle but does not show it on a basket. It is true that the trapezoid appears in the haxpo'o waxpo'o design, but it is apparently not an essential element. At any rate it is not found singly.

The diamond, as a single element, constitutes a modified form of both snake-nose and sturgeon-back designs, but there is no instance in basketry in which a double row of isosceles triangles forms a row of bisected diamonds. Likewise, the complete diamond seems not to occur in a row with apices touching.

The acute isosceles triangle does not occur in basketry, although it is undoubtedly the favorite engraving motif. This is perhaps owing to the limitation of technique. That is, in basketry one builds a triangle by the consecutive increase or decrease of a stitch on one or both sides, automatically forming a right-angled or obtuse triangle, the twined stitch being longer than high.

Some of the basket designs, however, do occur in carving. The flint, sharp-tooth, sturgeon-back, and crooked patterns are all found. Plate 113*d* shows the direct transfer of the basketry "spread finger" design to engraving, yet this sort of direct transfer is not frequent. Of course elements as simple as the triangle and zigzag are bound to occur in identical form. The rectangle is lacking in the engraving, which suggests that it may be an outgrowth of the textile technique.

In general, basketry designs are more varied and complex than those of carving. None of the intricate textile designs are copied in engraving, although that might well have been done. The waxpo'o, foot, elk, striped designs, and many combinations have no counterpart in the incising. However, as one would expect, the correspondence between the basketry and purse decoration is more pronounced than between the basketry and spoon and paddle decoration.

---

13 Based on Kroeber, Basket Designs of the Indians of Northwestern California, UC–PAAE, 4:105–164, 1905.

14 Goddard, Life and Culture of the Hupa, UC–PAAE, 4:1, fig. 6, 1904.

GENERAL SUMMARY

Broadly speaking, the art of these peoples is fairly uniform. Considering the differences in material and size, there is a surprising degree of similarity between the spoon and the paddle. The purse, too, adheres to the same sort of design elements, although it calls for engraving rather than sculpture. The basketry decoration also conforms to a considerable extent.

It is safe to declare that the carving art of northwestern California is purely geometric, unsymbolic, and dominated by the triangle and zigzag. The triangle is probably the more fundamental of the two. The sketch below (fig. 7) shows how triangles may combine to form a zigzag. The first two are basketry designs, and the last is a purse engraving.

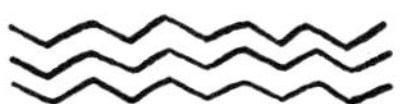
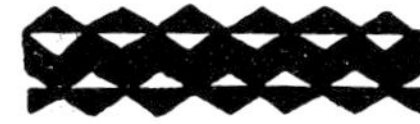

Fig. 7. Triangular and zigzag motifs.

Furthermore, it is plain that this art is distinctive from that of most of California, where carving is absent and where basketry design is the chief form of aesthetic expression. It differs fundamentally from the art of the North Pacific Coast which is dominated by conventionalized human and animal motives. It lacks also the symbolism of the Northwest Coast.

It is interesting to note that this specialized type of decoration has been applied to three principal objects, each of diverse origin. Spoon manufacture perhaps received its initial impulse from the North Pacific Coast, although the finished product is quite different; the mush paddle is undoubtedly an elaboration of the simple California implement; and the horn purse is a local invention.

EXPLANATION OF PLATES

Below are given the specimen numbers and provenance of objects illustrated. The sequence is from left to right unless otherwise specified.

Plate 103. Elk-horn spoons, Klamath river. *a*, 1–1237, height of stem, 15 cm.; *b*, 1–1238.

Plate 104. Elk-horn spoons, Klamath river. *a*, 1–1241, height of stem, 12 cm.; *b*, 1–1240.

Plate 105. Elk-horn spoons, Yurok. *a*, 1–1974, woman's spoon; *b*, 1–9429; *c*, 1–1938; *d*, 1–11573, height of stem, 10.8 cm.; others on same scale; *e*, 1–1103; *f*, 1–1308.

Plate 106. Elk-horn spoons. *a*, 1–1303, Yurok; *b*, 1–1068, Yurok, height of stem, 14 cm.; others on same scale; *c*, 1–2113, Yurok; *d*, 1–2355, Hupa; *e*, 1–1118, Yurok; *f*, 1–1112, Yurok; *g*, 1–2069, Yurok; *h*, 1–1943, Yurok; *i*, 1106, Yurok; *j*, 1–2219, Yurok; *k*, 1–845, Hupa; *l*, 1–1099, Yurok.

Plate 107. Elk-horn spoons. *a*, 1–1104, Yurok, height of stem, 5.8 cm.; others on same scale; *b*, 1–2031, Yurok; *c*, 1–1993, Yurok; *d*, 1–2030, Yurok; *e*, 1–849, Hupa; *f*, 1–1236, Klamath river; *g*, 1–1241, Klamath river; *h*, 1–1240, Klamath river; *i*, 1–1937, Yurok; *j*, 1–1875, Yurok; *k*, 1–2347, Hupa; *l*, 1–1986, Yurok.

Plate 108. Elk-horn spoons. *a*, 1–4444, Klamath river; *b*, 1–106, Klamath river, height of stem, 10.5 cm.; others on same scale; *c*, 1–2348, Hupa; *d*, 1–792, Hupa; *e*, 1–1238, Klamath river; *f*, 1–1237, Klamath river; *g*, 1–791, Hupa; *h*, 1–794, Hupa; *i*, 1–2028, Yurok; *j*, 1–1239, Klamath river; *k*, 1–2226, Yurok; *l*, 1–1316, Yurok.

Plate 109. Wooden mush paddles. *a*, 1–820, Hupa, height, 75 cm.; *b*, *c*, *d* on same scale; *b*, 1–1911, Yurok; *c*, 1–821, Hupa; *d*, 1–882, Hupa; *e*, 1–9471, Yurok, height, 81.5 cm.; *f*, *g*, *h* on same scale; *f*, 1–1633, Yurok; *g*, 1–2188, Yurok; *h*, 1–11828, Yurok.

Plate 110. Wooden mush paddles, Yurok. *a*, 1–2198, height, 92.5 cm.; *b*, *c*, *d* on same scale; *b*, 1–1860; *c*, 1–1891; *d*, 1–1833; *e*, 1–1618, height, 76.5 cm.; *f*, *g*, *h* on same scale; *f*, 1–2192; *g*, 1–2194; *h*, 1–2193.

Plate 111. Wooden mush paddles. *a*, 1–1647, Yurok; *b*, 1–819, Hupa, height 64 cm.; *a*, *c*, *d*, *e* on same scale; *c*, 1–1611, Yurok; *d*, 1–1892, Yurok; *e*, 1–1948, Yurok; *f*, 1–2224, Yurok, height, 87.5 cm.; *g*, *h*, *i* on same scale; *g*, 1–1563, Yurok; *h*, 1–1640, Yurok; *i*, 1–1679, Yurok.

Plate 112. Wooden mush paddles. *a*, 1–2002, Yurok, height, 100 cm.; others on same scale; *b*, 1–862, Hupa; *c*, 1–2001, Yurok; *d*, 1–2035, Yurok.

Plate 113. Elk-horn purses. *a*, 1–1562, Yurok; *b*, 1–2278, probably Yurok; *c*, 1–2286, probably Yurok, length, 9.2 cm.; others on same scale; *d*, 1–1427, Yurok.

Plate 114. Elk-horn purses. *a*, 1–2284, probably Yurok, length, 15.6 cm.; others on same scale; *b*, 1–914, Hupa; *c*, 1–2288a, probably Yurok; *d*, 1–2068, Yurok.

Plate 115. Elk-horn purses. *a*, 1–1219, Yurok, length, 14.5 cm.; others on same scale; *b*, 1–810, Hupa; *c*, 1–9482, Yurok.

Plate 116. Elk-horn purses. *a*, 1–2283, probably Yurok; *b*, 1–1560, Yurok; *c*, 1–1222, Yurok, length, 10.3 cm.; others on same scale; *d*, lid to *c*.

Plate 117. Elk-horn purses, Yurok, except *d* and *e*. *a*, 1–4425; *b*, 1–1220; *c*, 1223ab; *d*, 1–1251, Klamath river; *e*, specimen lost; *f*, 1–1221ab; *g*, 1–1222; *h*, 1–1149; *i*, 1–1145; *j*, 1–1148; *k*, 1–1150; *l*, 1–1151, height, including lid, 9.5 cm.; others on same scale.

Plate 118. *a*, entrance to sacred house, Takimitlding village, Hupa; *b*, 1–1555ab, wooden box, Yurok, length, 105 cm.; *c*, 1–2020, wooden box, Yurok, length, 46 cm.

Plate 119. Various objects, all Yurok but *i*. *a*, 1–2023, netting shuttle, length, 28 cm.; others on same scale; *b*, 1–1944, woman's spoon; *c*, 1–2144, mesh measure; *d*, 1–2138, mesh measure; *e*, 1–2092, mesh measure; *f*, 1–2189, hairpin; *g*, 1–11817d, hairpin; *h*, 1–9532, girl's head-scratcher; *i*, 1–1246, Klamath river, "louse killer"; *j*, 1–1573, strung dentalia, ornamented.

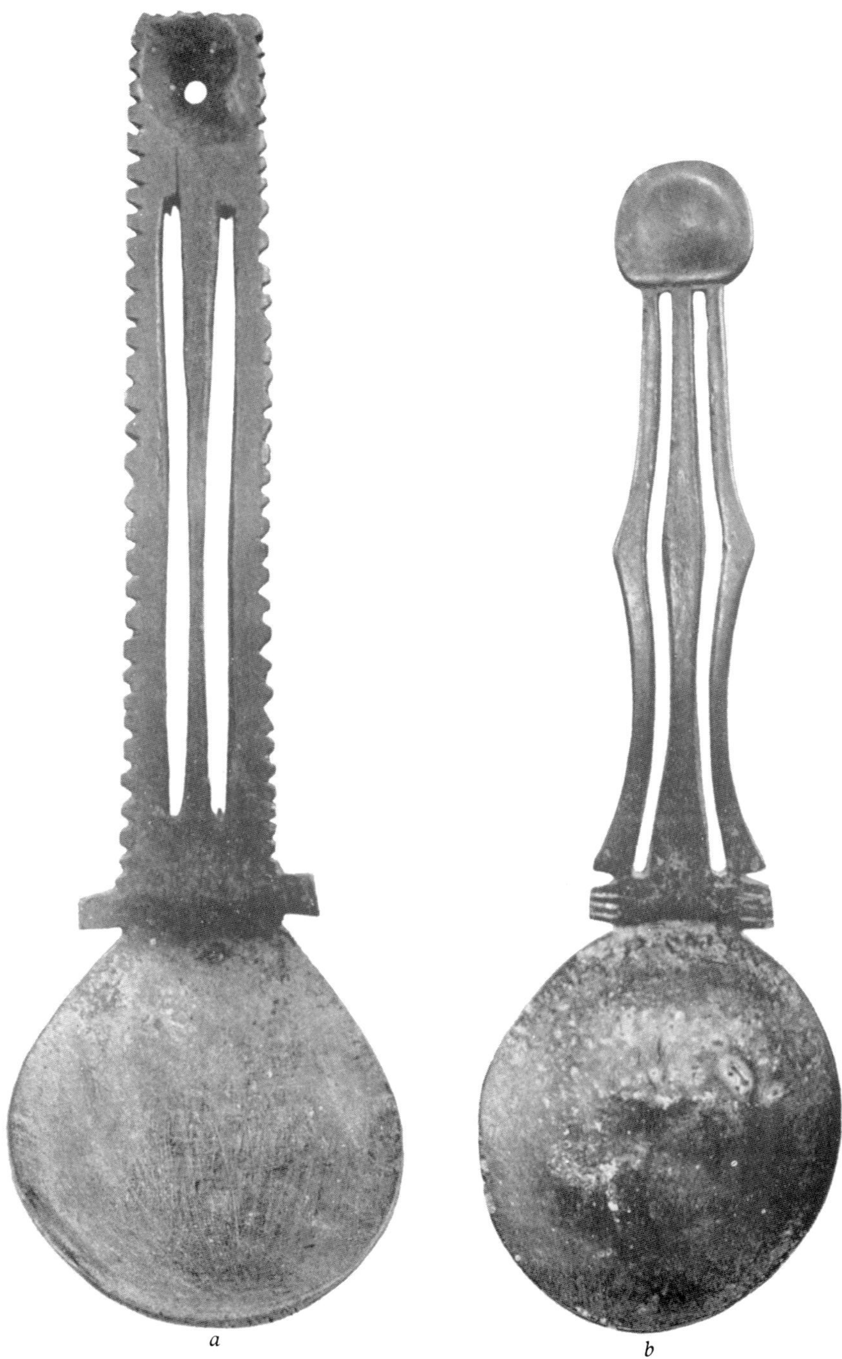

a *b*

ELK-HORN SPOONS

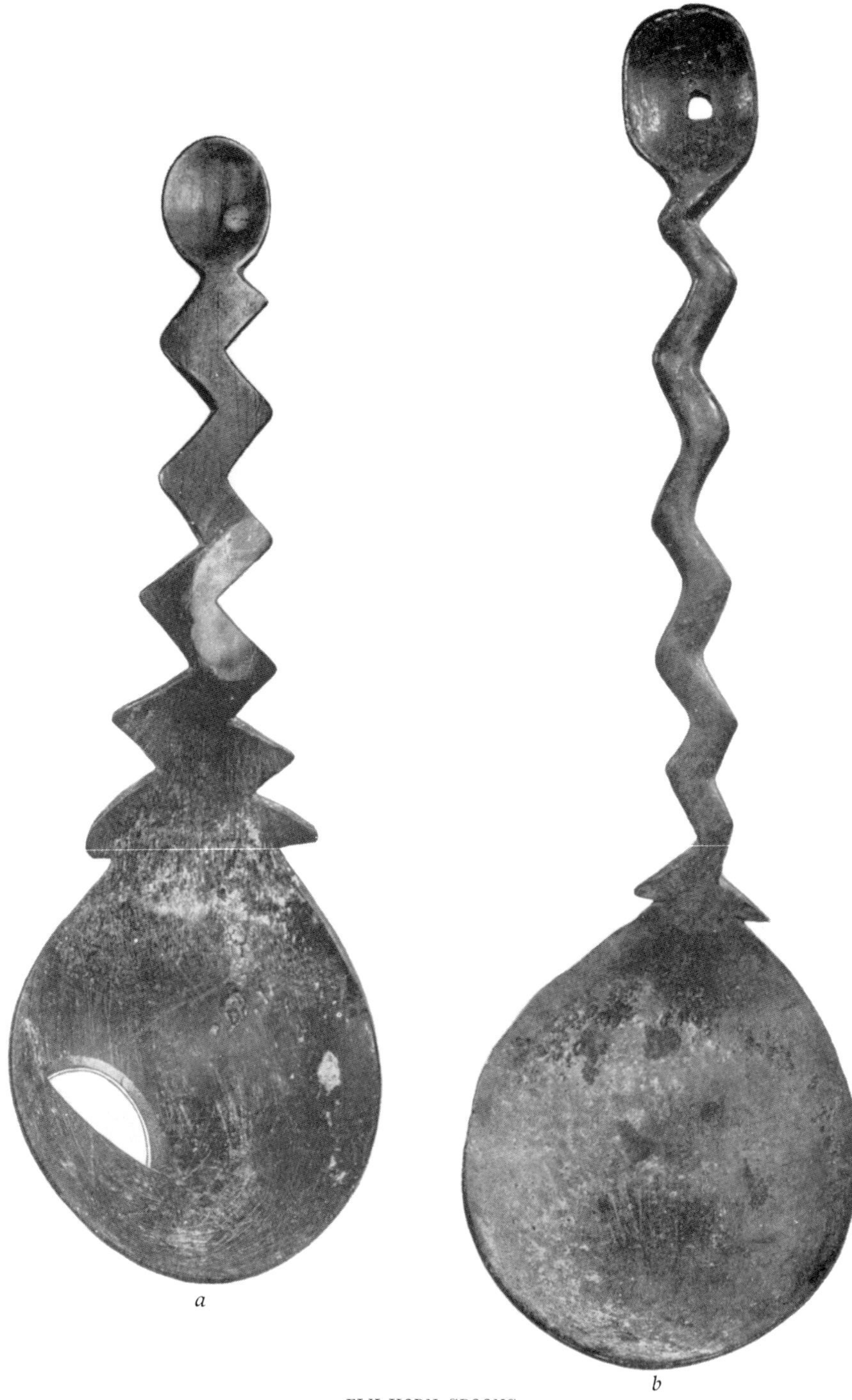

ELK-HORN SPOONS

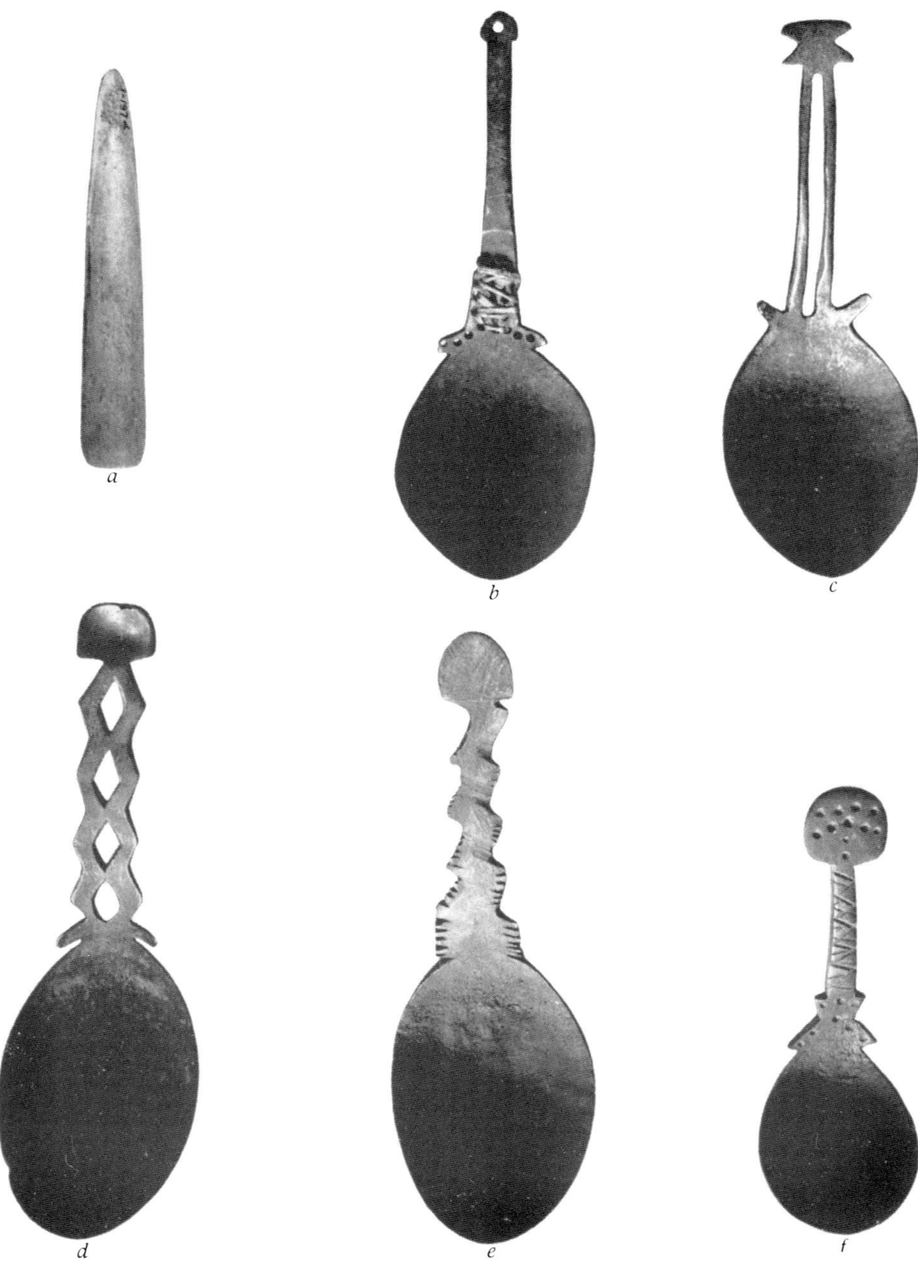

ELK-HORN SPOONS

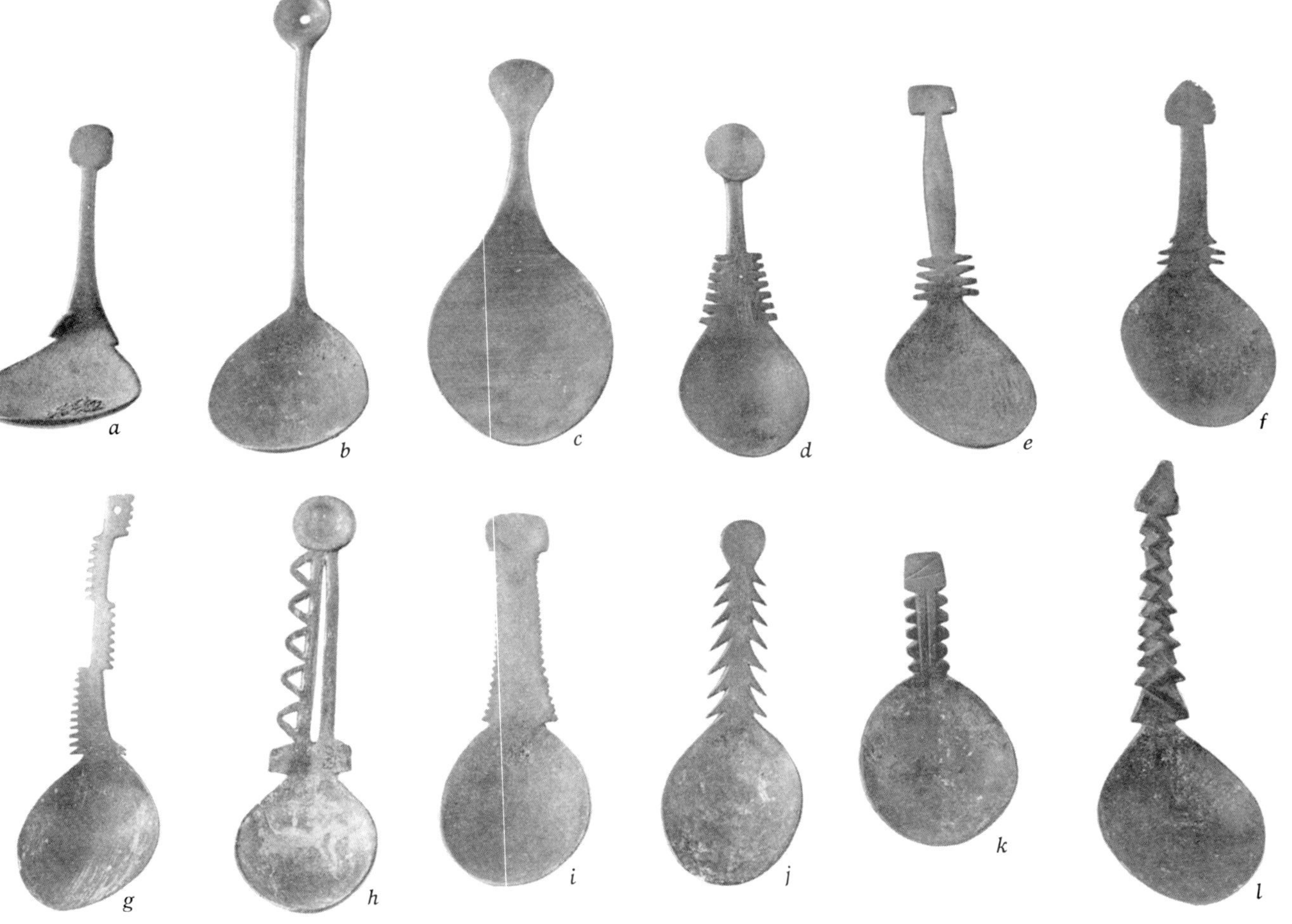

ELK-HORN SPOONS

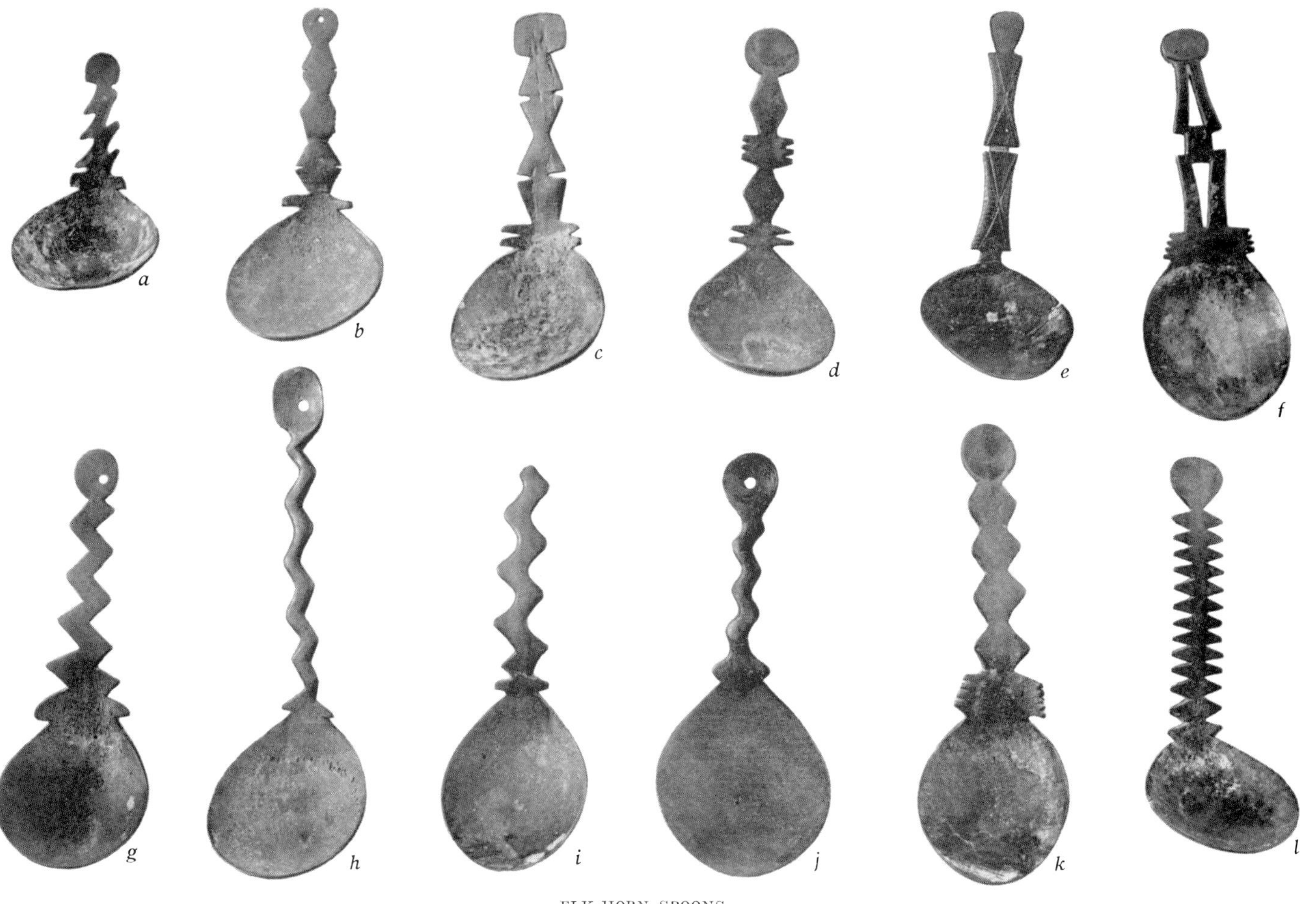

ELK-HORN SPOONS

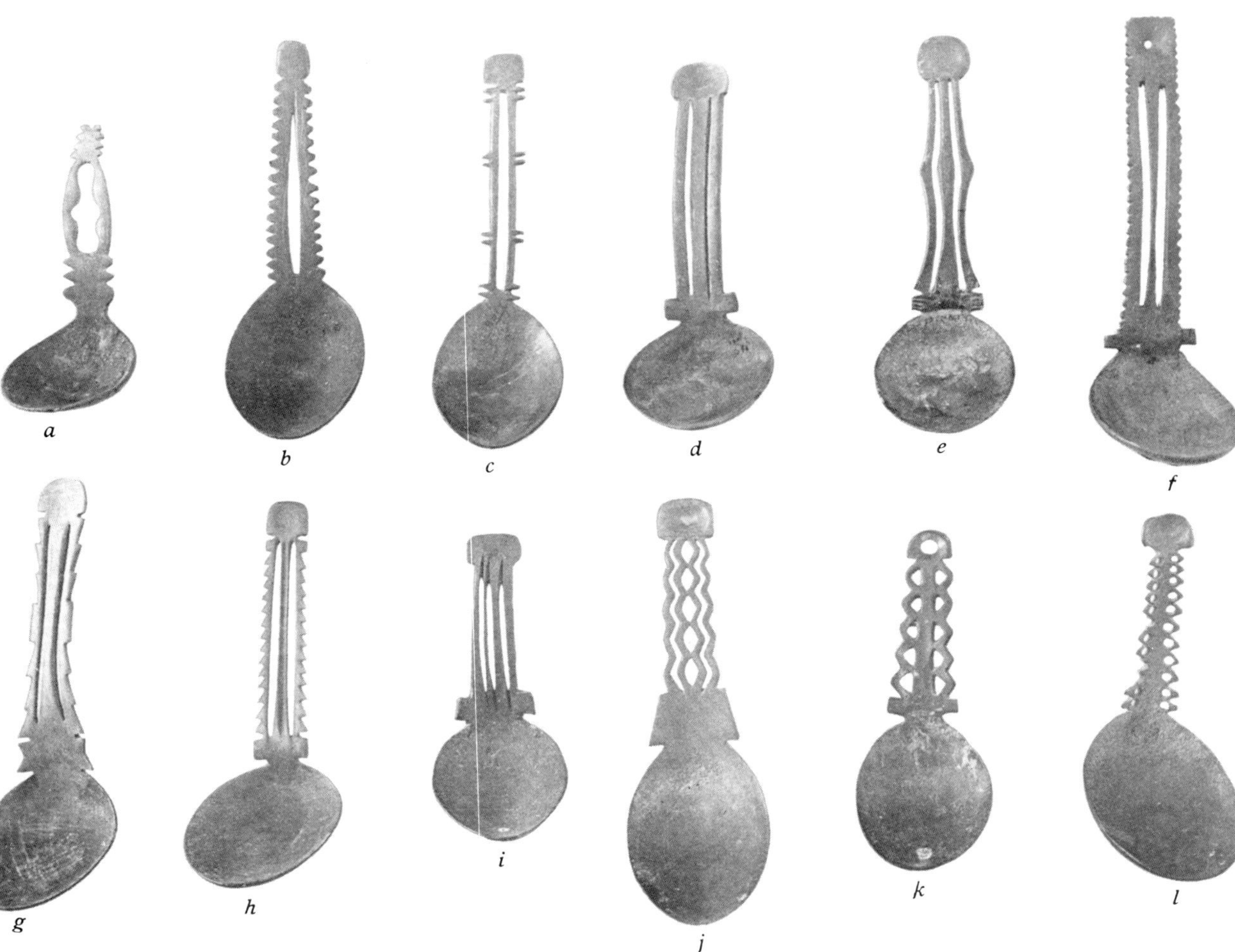

ELK-HORN SPOONS

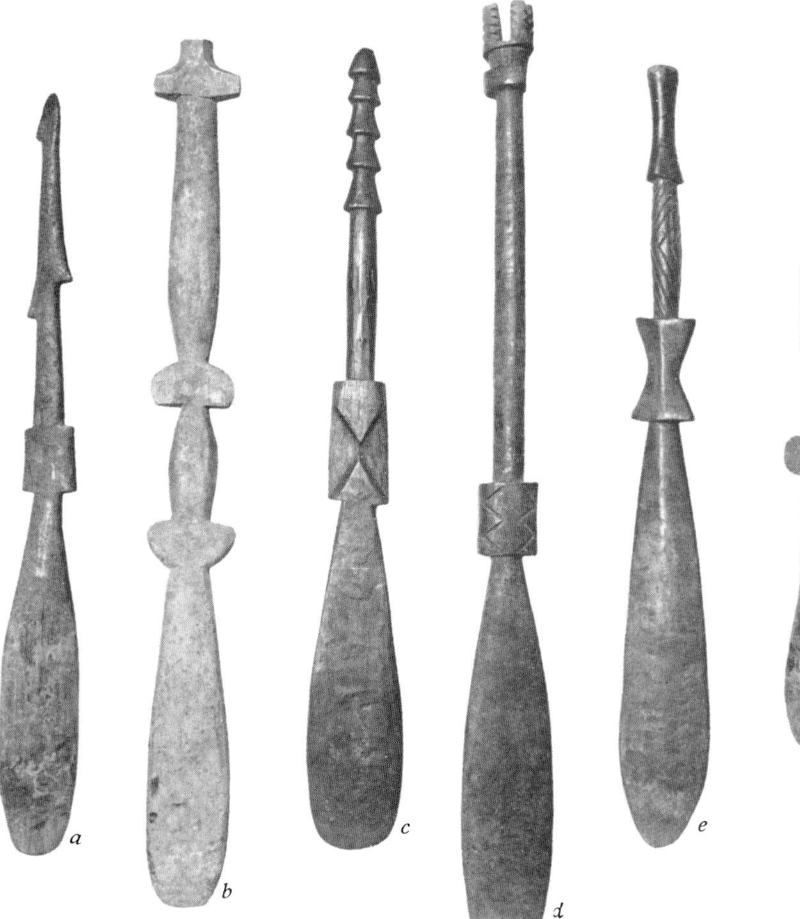

WOODEN MUSH PADDLES

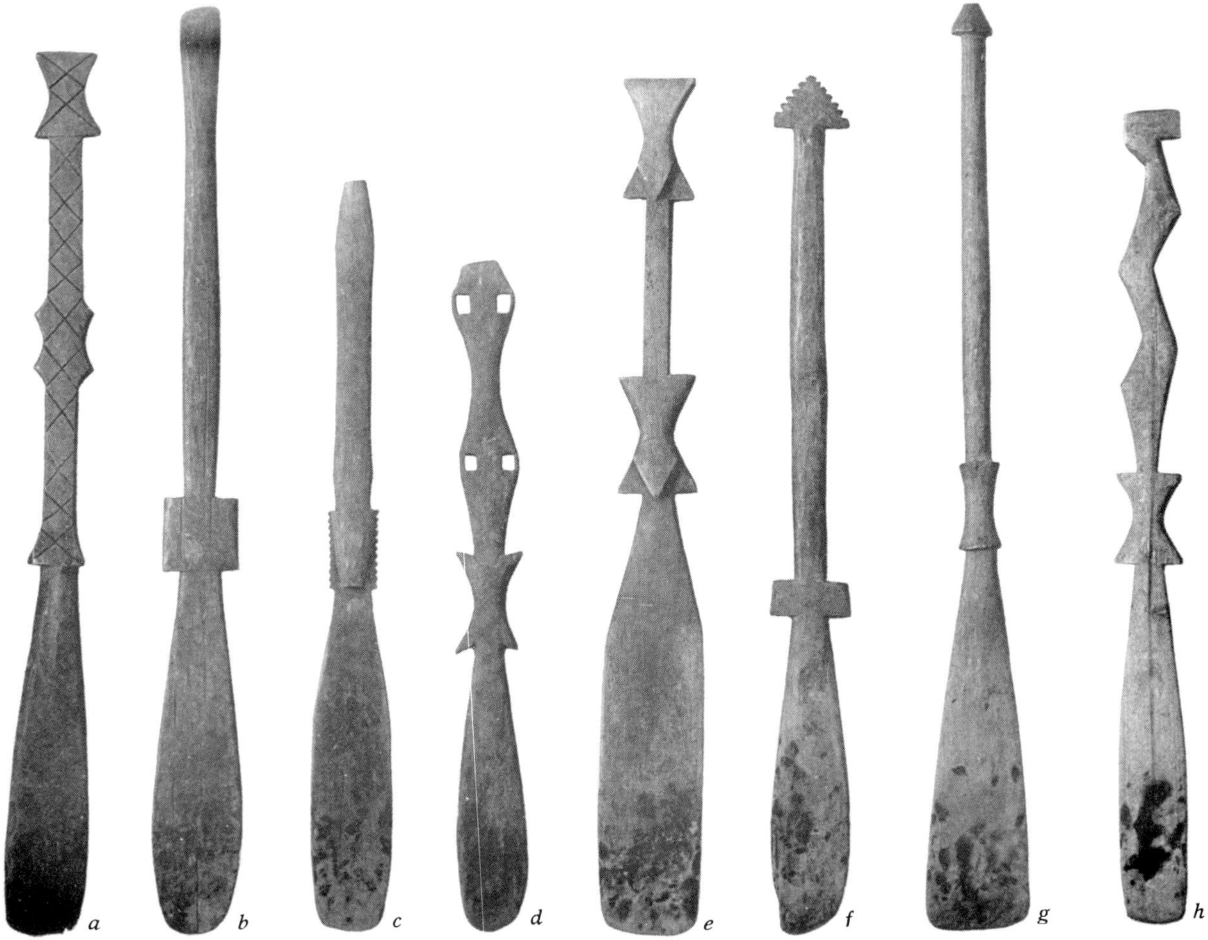

WOODEN MUSH PADDLES

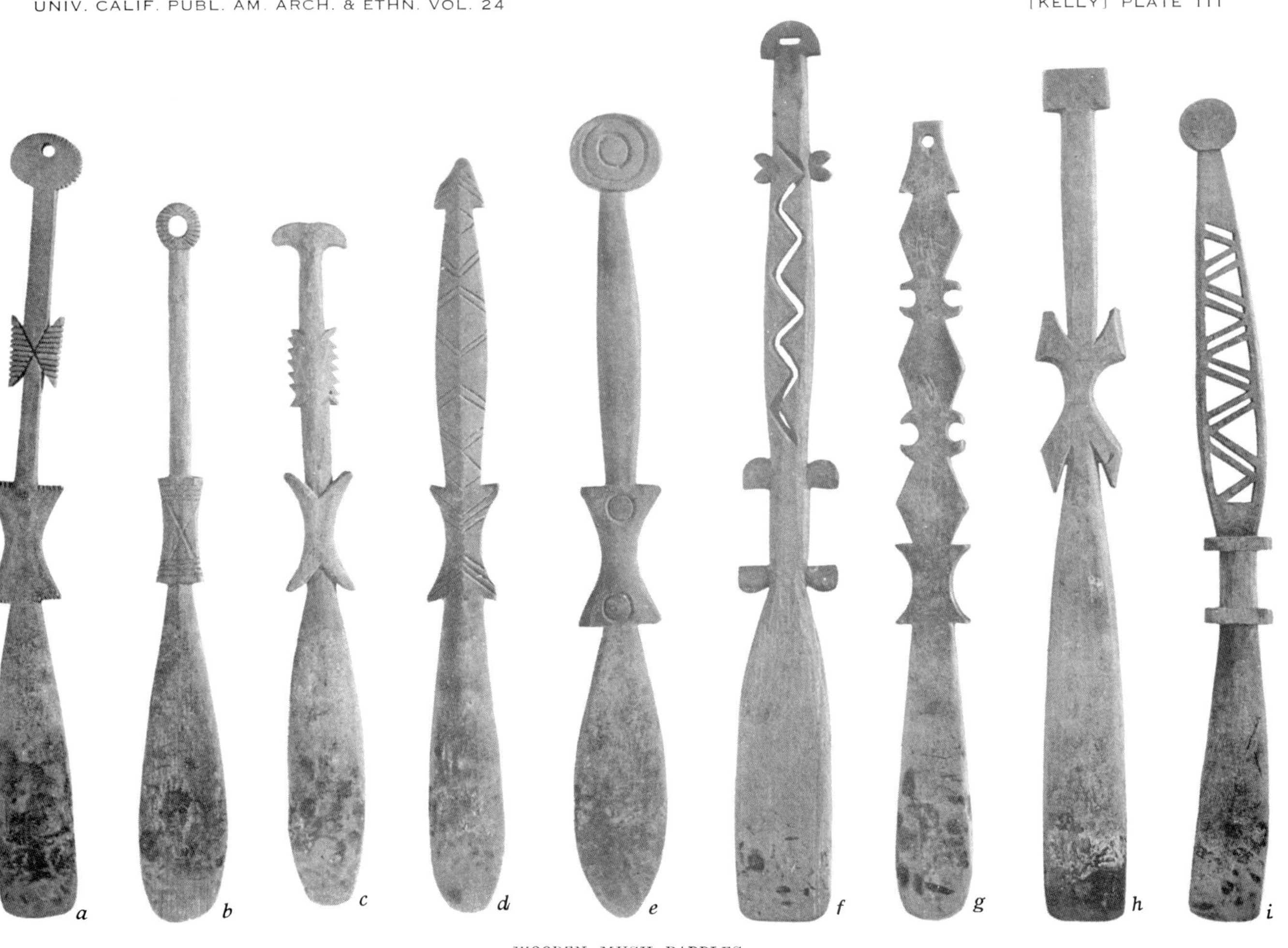

WOODEN MUSH PADDLES

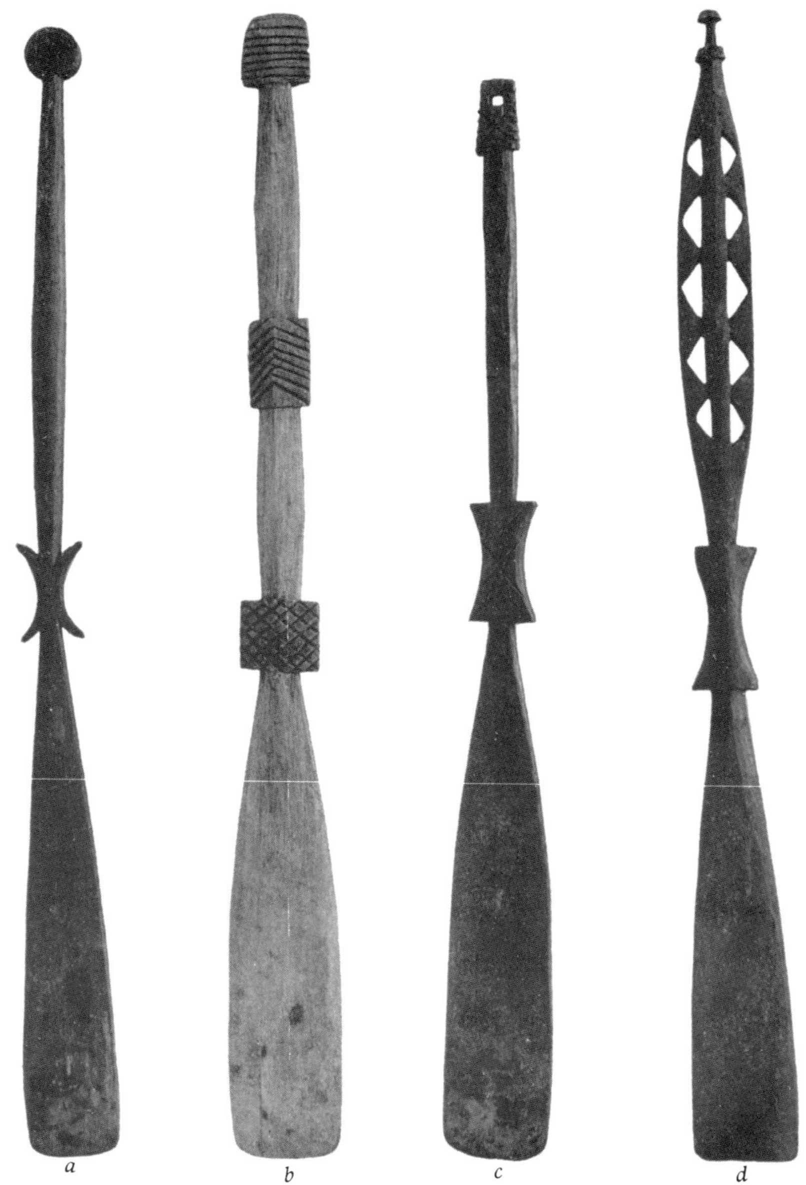

WOODEN MUSH PADDLES

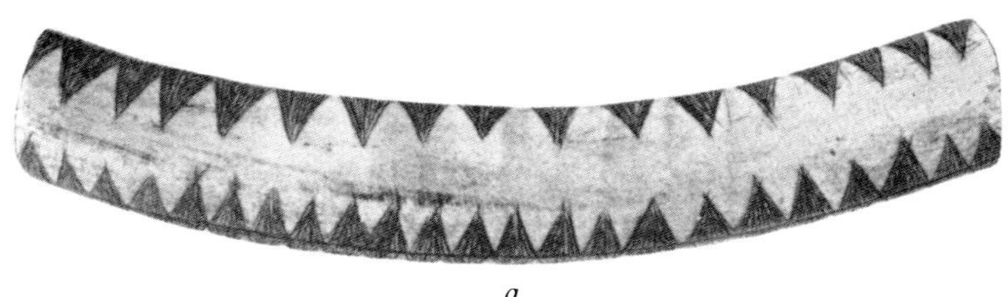

a

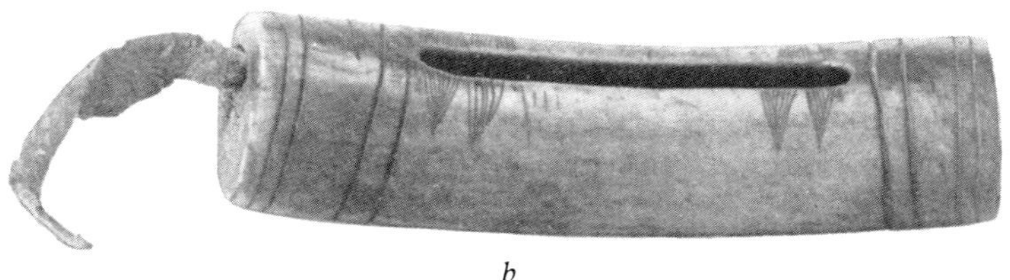

b

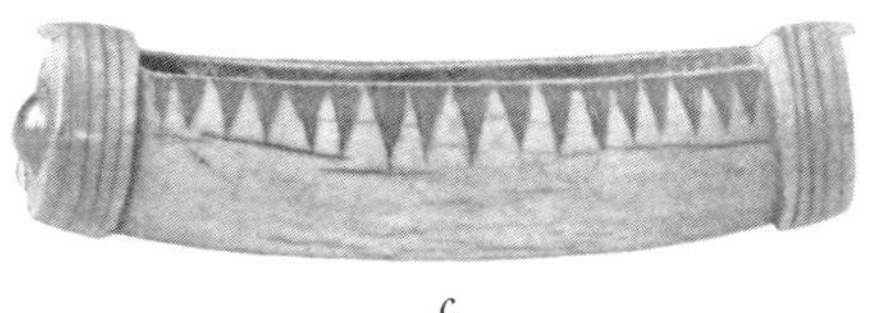

c

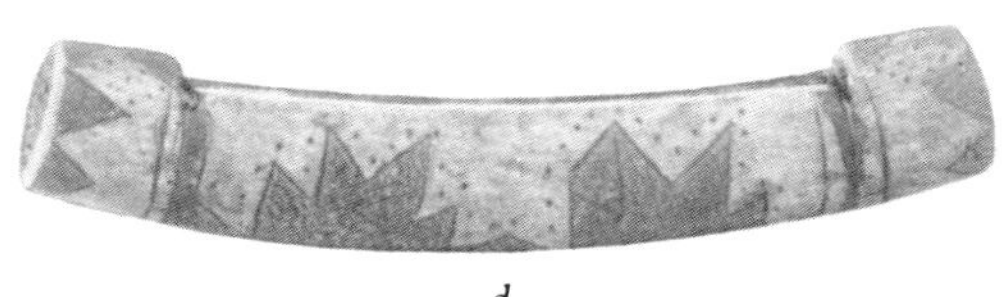

d

ELK-HORN PURSES

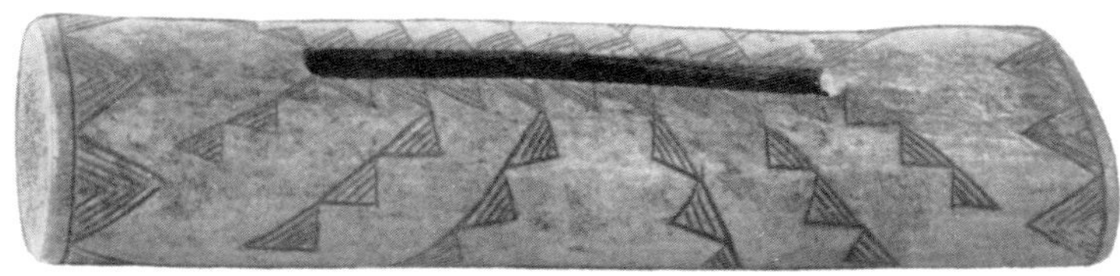

a

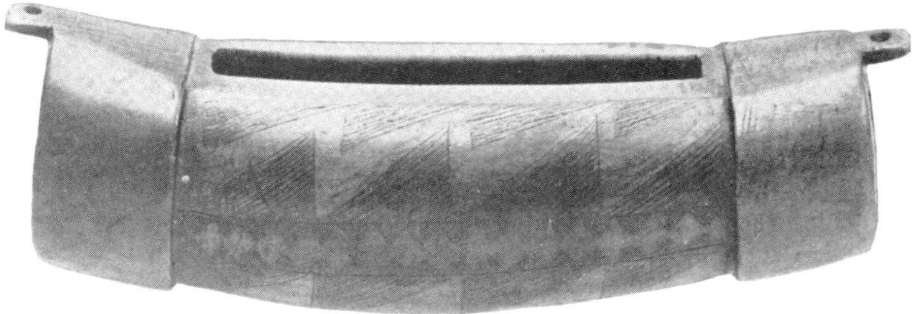

b

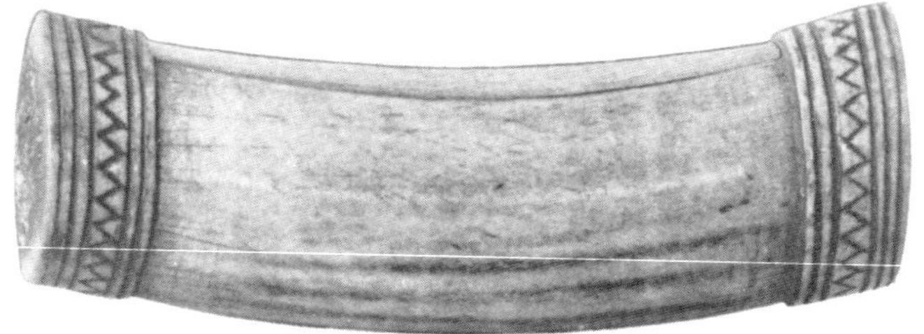

c

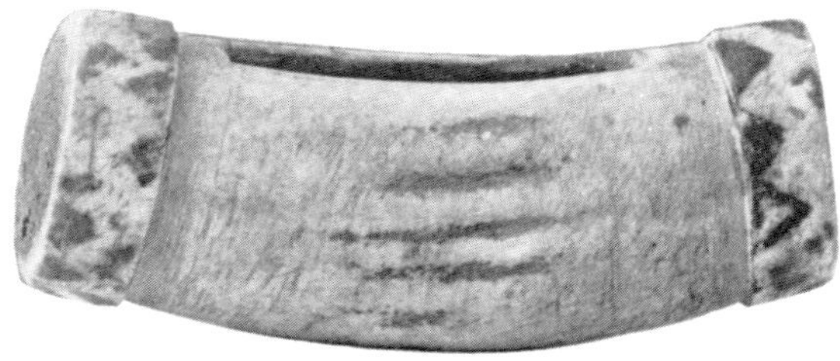

d

ELK-HORN PURSES

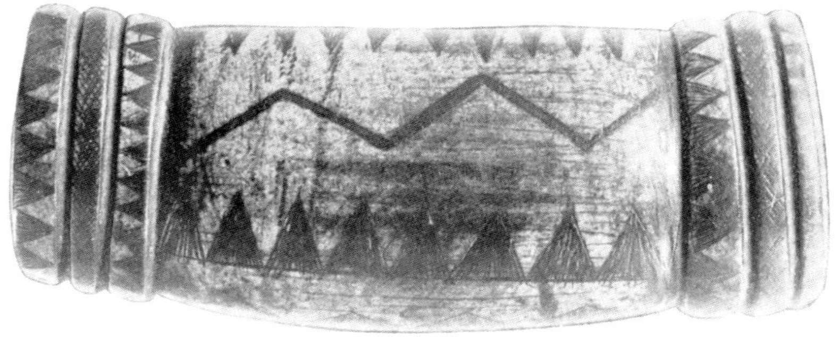

a

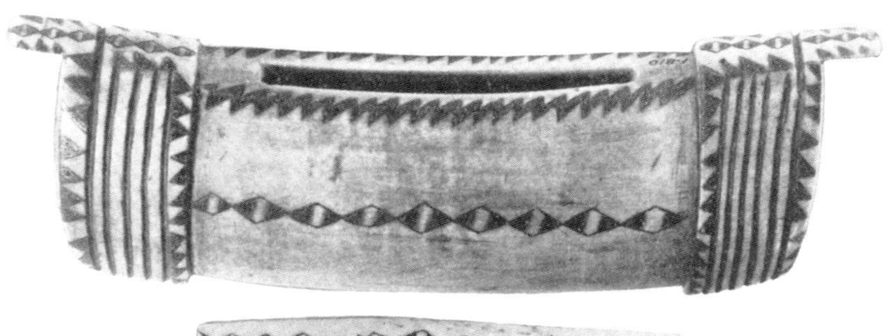

b

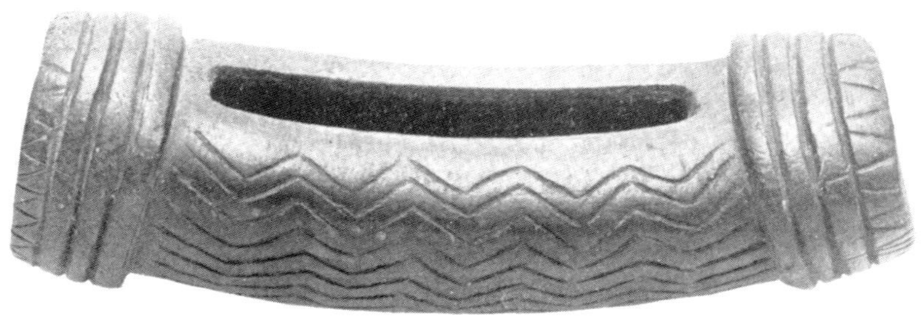

c

ELK-HORN PURSES

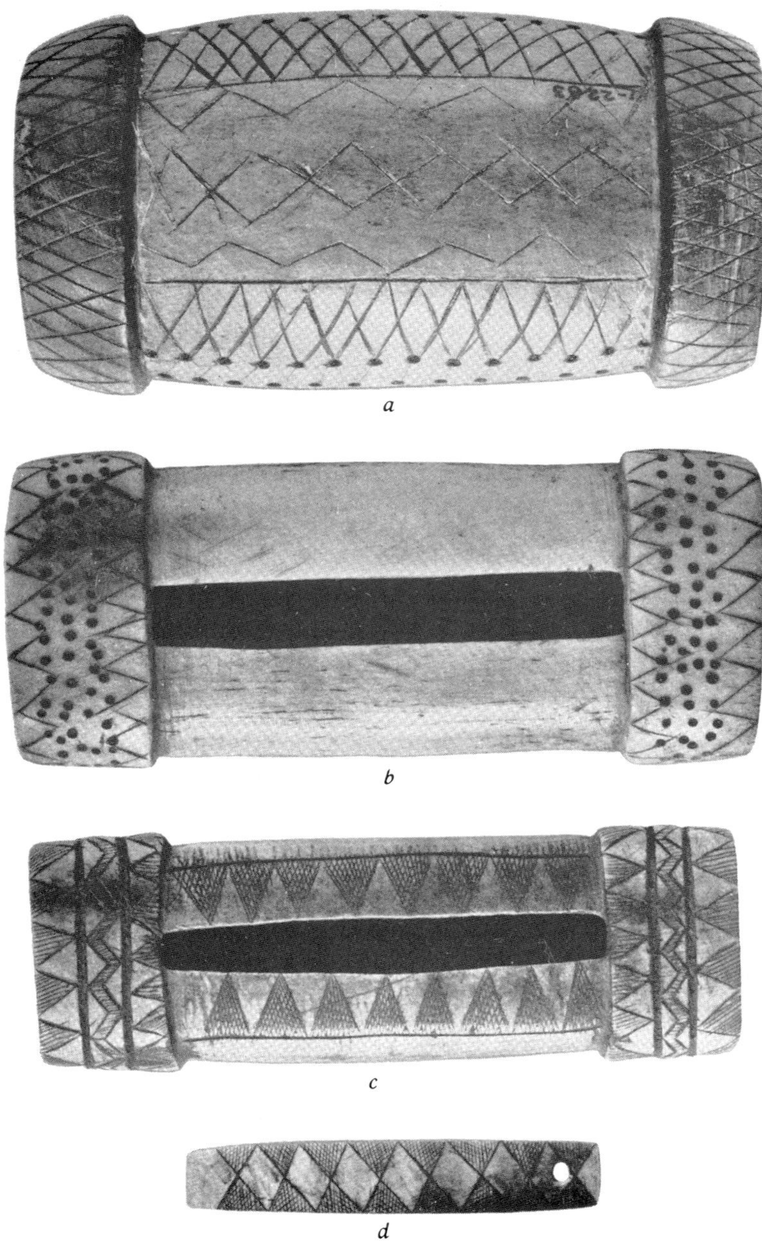

ELK-HORN PURSES

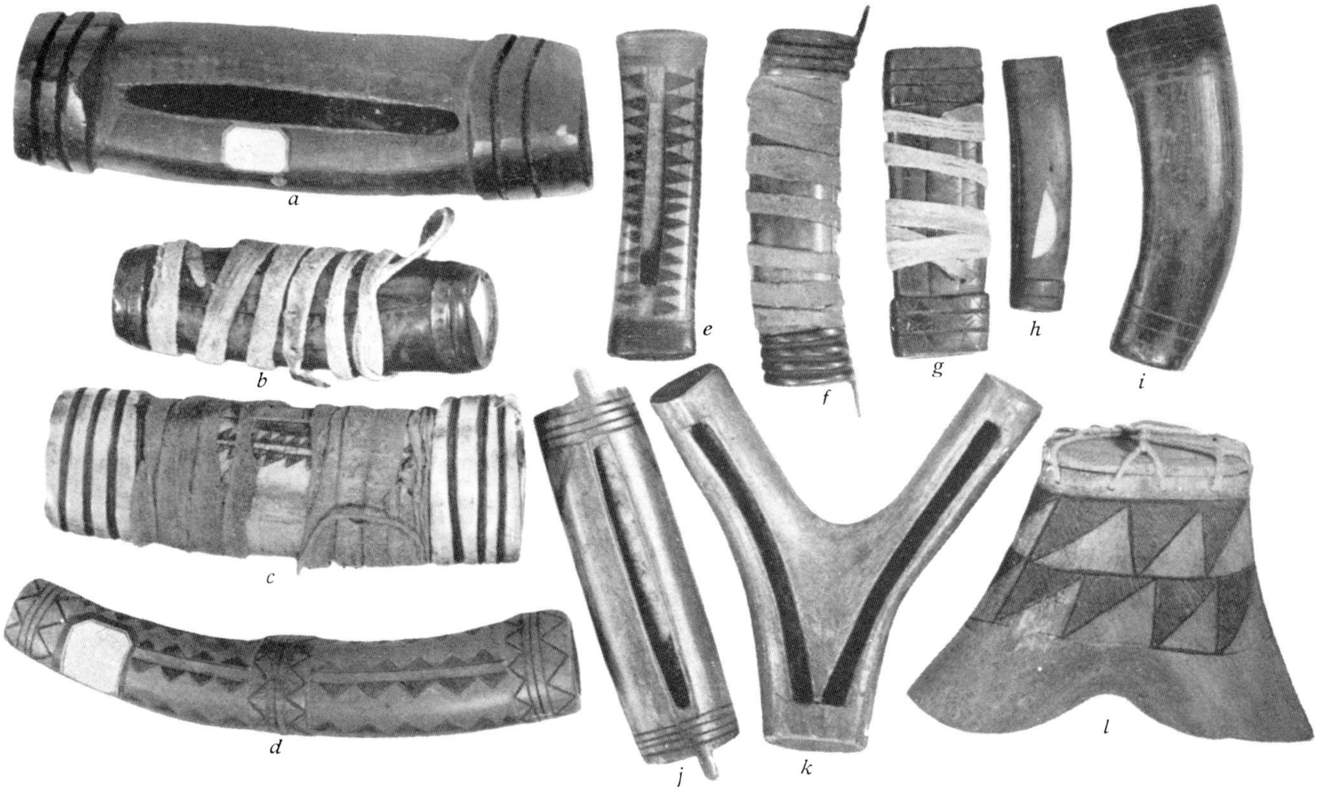

ELK-HORN PURSES

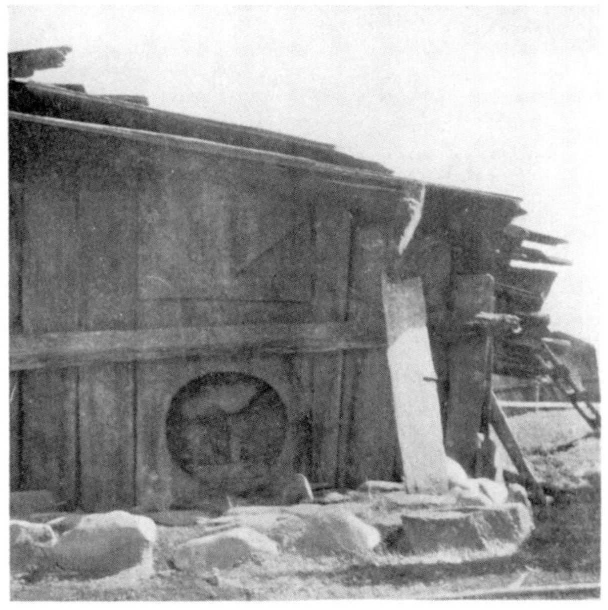

a

b

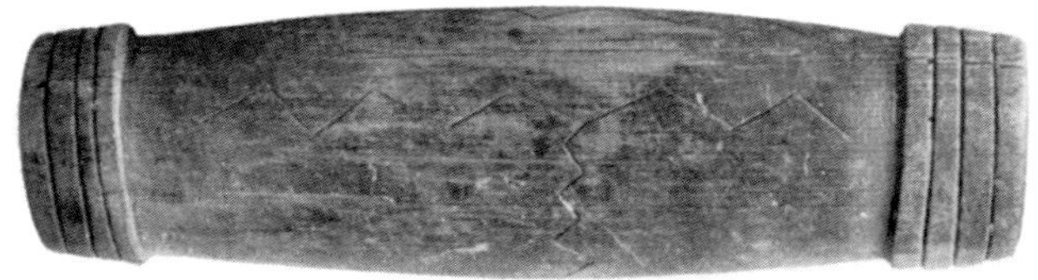

c

SACRED HOUSE, HUPA; WOODEN STORAGE BOXES

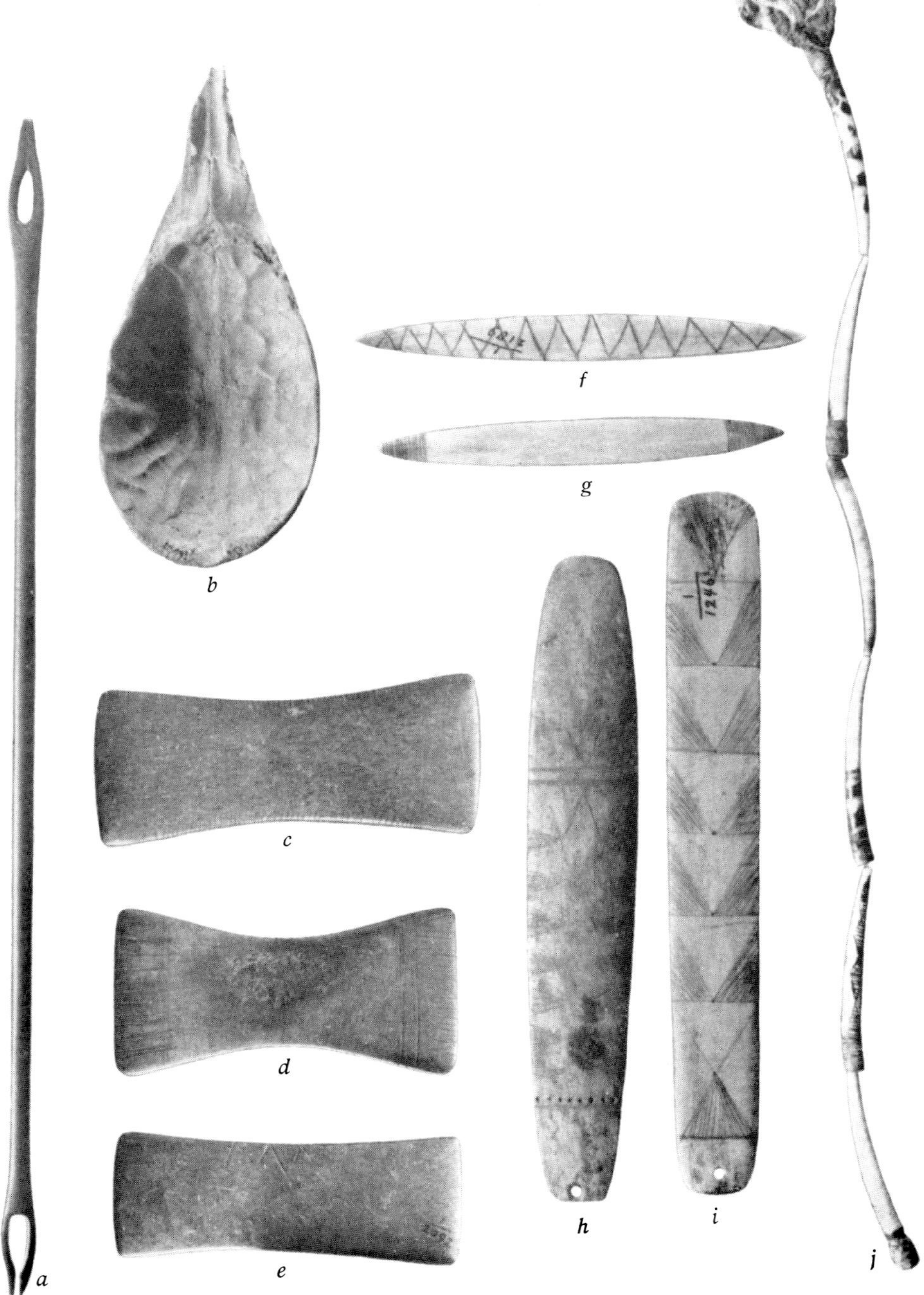

OBJECTS OF BONE, HORN, AND SHELL

ABBREVIATIONS USED

A	Anthropos.
l'A	L'Anthropologie.
AA	American Anthropologist.
AAA-M	American Anthropological Association, Memoirs.
ArA	Archiv für Anthropologie.
AES-P	American Ethnological Society, Publications.
AGW-M	Anthropologische Gesellschaft in Wien, Mitteilungen.
AJPA	American Journal of Physical Anthropology.
AMNH	American Museum of Natural History—
-AP	Anthropological Papers.
-B	Bulletin.
-M	Memoirs.
-MA	Memoirs, Anthropological Series.
-MJ	Memoirs, Jesup Expedition.
BAE	Bureau of American Ethnology—
-B	Bulletins.
-R	(Annual) Reports.
CNAE	Contributions to North American Ethnology.
CU-CA	Columbia University, Contributions to Anthropology.
FL	Folk–Lore.
FMNH	Field Museum of Natural History—
-M	Memoirs.
-PAS	Publications, Anthropological Series.
IAE	Internationales Archiv für Ethnographie.
ICA	International Congress of Americanists (Comptes Rendus, Proceedings).
IJAL	International Journal of American Linguistics.
JAFL	Journal of American Folk-Lore.
JRAI	Journal of the Royal Anthropological Institute.
MAIHF	Museum of the American Indian, Heye Foundation—
-C	Contributions.
-IN	Indian Notes.
-INM	Indian Notes and Monographs.
PM	Peabody Museum (of Harvard University)—
-M	Memoirs.
-P	Papers.
-R	Reports.
PMM-B	Public Museum (of the City) of Milwaukee, Bulletin.
SAP-J	Société des Américanistes de Paris, Journal.
SI	Smithsonian Institution—
-AR	Annual Reports.
-CK	Contributions to Knowledge.
-MC	Miscellaneous Collections.
UC-PAAE	University of California, Publications in American Archaeology and Ethnology.
UPM-AP	University of Pennsylvania (University) Museum, Anthropological Publications.
USNM	United States National Museum—
-R	Reports.
-P	Proceedings.
UW-PA	University of Washington, Publications in Anthropology.
ZE	Zeitschrift für Ethnologie.

ABOUT THE AUTHORS

IRA JACKNIS, Associate Research Anthropologist at the Phoebe Hearst Museum, is a specialist in the Native arts and cultures of Western North America. With artists George Blake (Hupa/Yurok) and Frank Gist (Yurok), he is co-curator of the associated exhibition, "The Carver's Art of the Indians of Northwestern California" (Hearst Museum, August 23–1995–February 4, 1996).

ISABEL TRUESDELL KELLY (1906–1982) was an archaeologist specializing in West Mexican prehistory. She was also known for her research on Southwestern archaeology, Great Basin ethnography, public health, and Mexican social anthropology. "The Carver's Art of the Indians of Northwestern California" was her 1927 Master's paper (anthropology at the University of California, Berkeley).